THE WEEKEND CHEF

The

WEEKEND
CHEF EASY
FOOD FOR
LAZY DAYS
CATHERINE
FULVIO

GILL & MACMILLAN

Gill & Macmillan
Hume Avenue
Park West
Dublin 12
with associated companies throughout the world
www.gillmacmillanbooks.ie

© Catherine Fulvio 2013

978 07171 5861 4

Design by www.grahamthew.com
Photography © Joanne Murphy
Photographer's assistant: Líosa Mac Namara
Stylists: Carly Horan and Blondie Horan
Edited by Kristin Jensen
Indexed by Cliff Murphy
Printed by Printer Trento Srl, Italy

This book is typeset in 10 on 14pt Whitney.

Props
Ashley Cottage Interiors, Tralee, Co. Kerry;
Arnotts, Henry St, Dublin 1: www.arnotts.ie, Tel: (01) 805 0400;
Avoca, Rathcoole, Co. Dublin: www.avoca.ie, Tel: (01) 257 1800;
Historic Interiors, Oberstown, Lusk, Co. Dublin: Tel: (01) 843 7174, E: killian@historicinteriors.net;
Meadows & Byrne, Dún Laoghaire, Co. Dublin: Tel: (01) 280 4554;
Two Wooden Horses, Chapel Rd, Greystones, Wicklow: Tel: (083) 405 6492,
E: twowoodenhorses@gmail.com

The paper used in this book comes from the wood pulp of managed forests. For every tree felled, at least
one tree is planted, thereby renewing natural resources.

A CIP catalogue record for this book is available from the British Library.

CATHERINE FULVIO is the proprietor of Ballyknocken House & Cookery School, Co. Wicklow, and one of Ireland's top television culinary stars. Her previous books, *Catherine's Italian Kitchen*, *Catherine's Family Kitchen* and *Eat Like an Italian*, were all bestsellers. *Eat Like an Italian* was the winner of the Irish Cookbook of the Year at the 2012 Bord Gáis Energy Irish Book Awards. Born and raised in Ireland and married to an Italian, Catherine's books always reflect this match made in heaven by using easily accessible Irish ingredients assembled with an Italian flair. Catherine is now a regular guest on BBC One's *Saturday Kitchen*. This book is inspired by one of Catherine's most popular courses at Ballyknocken, *The Weekend Chef*.

Acknowledgements

I am blessed to find myself working with such a great bunch of colleagues and friends. We have been together for many years now. So thank you to all the team here at Ballyknocken House & Cookery School. Thank you especially to Sharon for your inspiration and dedication and thank you to Ella for your kitchen magic.

Thanks also to the photographic and prop team, who I'm sure you will agree did and amazing job – grazie to Jo, Carly, Lisa and Blondie.

And thank you to all at Gill & Macmillan, especially to Nicki for your fantastic enthusiasm and vision. And thank you to Kristin for your patience too. Many thanks to Catherine, Teresa, Paul, Peter and Graham for your dedication to *The Weekend Chef*.

And thank you to my husband, Claudio, and the junior chefs that are Charlotte and Rowan. You are the sunshine that makes me grow.

But my biggest thank you is kept for last. Thank you to my dad, Charlie, and my late mother, Mary, for introducing me to this wonderful way of life: fresh food from the farm, an abundance of great ingredients and the knowledge to prepare them.

Grazie mile,
Catherine

Dedication

To my inspirational duo, Charlotte and Rowan –
my future weekend chefs!

{CONTENTS}

Ø3 <u>MOVIE NIGHT</u> Ø3

* * *

Ø4 <u>LATE LATE NIGHT SUPPER</u> Ø4

* * *

SATURDAY AFTERNOON
Ø5 <u>FOOD FOR THE MATCH</u> Ø5

Ø9 **DINNER PARTY** Ø9

* * *

(EASY LIKE) SUNDAY MORNING
1Ø SUNDAY BRUNCH 1Ø

A Healthy One

The Irish One

The Italiano

The All-American One

Scandi Style

Something to Drink

11 SUNDAY LUNCH 11

* * *

Introduction

'HAVE A GOOD WEEKEND!' HOW OFTEN DO WE THROW THIS IN AT THE END OF A CONVERSATION ON A FRIDAY? I DON'T KNOW ABOUT YOU, BUT LATELY I'VE BEEN FEELING THAT OUR WEEKENDS ARE IN DANGER OF BEING HOOVERED UP INTO THE WORKING WEEK.

Whether it's half an hour spent attempting to catch up on emails on a Friday night in front of the television or a portion of Sunday afternoon spent on paperwork, it increasingly seems like the work–life balance has become the work–life blend. Is that a good thing?

The Italians have a saying, 'Cuando l'amico chiede, non v'è domani', meaning 'When a friend asks, there is no tomorrow' – in other words, enjoy the moment now with friends. You would be hard pushed to find an Italian spending their precious family/free time in front of a computer screen. They would be at the beach or at the mountains, 'promenading' with an ice cream or enjoying dinners that go on for hours with copious amounts of food, family and friends.

And if weekends have a different vibe then, similarly, the weekends should be about a different kind of kitchen. If your kitchen during the week is like mine, it's a whirlwind of quick meals, bowls of cereal, homework being finished and planners being checked. To balance the hectic pace, the kitchen at the weekend should be about newspapers spread across half the table, feet up on the chairs, coffee brewing, French toast, baking, candlelit dinners, music, friends, family and laughter.

Start Friday after the play dates by watching a movie, making some yummy finger food or getting into your creative zone by making a curry from scratch.

Saturday morning begins and ends with brunch. Invite people over or just enjoy the relaxed time with your family. And if it's a rainy afternoon, how about closing the door, turning on the music and baking? It's such a good way to unwind.

And then on Sunday, rejoice in the sacred family time of Sunday lunch, the one day of the week where you guarantee a family get-together over good food and good times.

We all need to recharge, and we'll all be happier going back to the routine of Monday to Friday if we've spent the precious weekend unwinding. To help you get into the mood, I've suggested some great songs to cook to at the beginning of each chapter. So forget about the midweek humdrum. Forget about express meals. Close the door, turn the music on and fire up the cooker – it's the weekend!

Buon fine settimana – enjoy your weekend!

Catherine

FRIDAY NIGHT

'CHAN CHAN' – BUENA VISTA SOCIAL CLUB
....

'BROWN SUGAR' – THE ROLLING STONES
....

'(DO THE) MASHED POTATO' – JAMES BROWN
....

CHAPTER

01 } PLAY DATES

Our play date preference is usually a Friday afternoon or at the weekends now that the children are a little older. My friend and I often joke that we're so run off our feet with our children's social calendars that we need to organise our own play date for a chat and a coffee.

There is still that slight panic when time is not on my side, guests are checking into our B&B or I'm still teaching in the school and the play date friends need something to eat. I try my best to be organised a few days ahead of time. I ask my two for final numbers (once I arrived at school thinking that I would have one extra in the car and my son tried to get two more piled in; funny how kids arrange their own social life and forget to mention it to Mum!) and I also ask for food preferences: would a picnic in summer be a good idea or should we bake together, which is always a great hit?

1 TBSP EXTRA VIRGIN OLIVE OIL, PLUS EXTRA FOR FRYING

1 TSP GROUND CUMIN

1 TSP CHOPPED FRESH ROSEMARY

2 CHICKEN FILLETS, SLICED INTO STRIPS

SALT AND FRESHLY GROUND BLACK PEPPER

FOR THE SALAD:

2 MEDIUM CARROTS, PEELED AND SLICED INTO RIBBONS

½ CUCUMBER, PEELED AND SLICED INTO RIBBONS

¼ TSP CARAWAY SEEDS, TOASTED AND CRUSHED
  (OPTIONAL)

JUICE OF 1 LEMON (RESERVE A LITTLE TO DRIZZLE OVER
  THE AVOCADO, AS THIS PREVENTS IT FROM BROWNING)

4 TBSP EXTRA VIRGIN OLIVE OIL

1 TSP HONEY

SALT AND FRESHLY GROUND BLACK PEPPER

TO SERVE:

1 RIPE AVOCADO, PEELED, STONE REMOVED, THINLY
  SLICED AND DRIZZLED WITH LEMON JUICE

4 BAP ROLLS, SLICED IN HALF AND TOASTED

75G ROCKET OR ANY OF YOUR FAVOURITE SALAD LEAVES

SOUR CREAM (OPTIONAL)

1 To prepare the salad, place the carrot and cucumber ribbons in a bowl and add the caraway seeds. Whisk the lemon juice, oil and honey together and add in some salt and pepper. When ready to serve, pour over the salad and mix well.

2 Mix the oil, cumin and rosemary together and brush over the chicken, then season with salt and pepper. Allow to marinate for about 15 minutes. Heat some oil in a large frying pan or chargrill pan over a medium heat. Add the chicken strips and cook for 2-3 minutes on each side, depending on their size, until cooked through. Remove the chicken from the pan and set aside.

3 Arrange a few avocado slices in the bap rolls. Pack the chicken strips on top along with the carrot and cucumber salad and the rocket leaves. Drizzle over a little sour cream if you are using it.

CHICKEN AND CARROT SALAD BAPS

············

Fill the base of the baps with green leafy favourites so that they are out of sight and out of mind – no complaints of 'I don't like vegetables or salads!' from the younger crew.

SERVES 4

1 ROUNDED TSP DRIED YEAST (OR HALF A 7G SACHET)
½ TSP SUGAR
150ML LUKEWARM WATER (MORE IF REQUIRED)
250G ITALIAN '00' OR STRONG WHITE FLOUR
1 TSP EXTRA VIRGIN OLIVE OIL
½ TSP SALT
120ML GOOD-QUALITY TOMATO SAUCE

A FEW SUGGESTIONS FOR TOPPINGS:
• Chorizo, roasted red peppers and chargrilled asparagus
• Pancetta, spinach and feta
• Roasted courgette ribbons, aubergine and mozzarella
• Sliced mushrooms, roasted cherry tomatoes and shredded kale
• Leek, thin slices of sweet potatoes and roughly chopped walnuts
• For the sweet tooth – cream cheese, blueberries and raspberries
  with a maple syrup drizzle

MAKE YOUR OWN PIZZAS

. . . .

No matter what age you are, pizzas are popular! We have had some great fun making our own pizzas on Friday afternoons. I prepare the dough ahead of time and let it rise in a warm place. The toppings are in bowls so that everyone can choose what they like and have a go at creating their own. We have a time limit on creating the topping, and then into the hot oven they go.

MAKES TWO 30CM X 40CM RECTANGLES
OR TWO 30CM ROUNDS

1 To make the dough, mix the yeast and sugar in the lukewarm water and allow the yeast to activate. When the yeast foams, it's ready to use. This takes about 5 minutes.

2 Sieve the flour into a mixing bowl and add the olive oil, salt and the yeast mixture. Mix to a loose dough, adding more flour or water as required. Knead until the dough is very pliable, which should take about 5 minutes using the dough hook of a stand mixer or 7–10 minutes by hand. Leave the dough to rise in a well-oiled bowl covered with plastic wrap until the dough has trebled in size and is springy to the touch, which will take about 2 hours. This will rise best in a warm, draught-free place, e.g. a hot press or near an oven.

3 Preheat the oven to 230°C/fan 210°C /gas 7.

4 When the dough has risen, knock it back and place onto a lightly floured surface. Knead it again by hand for 2–3 minutes. Roll out or stretch the dough with your hands onto a lightly oiled pizza pan/screen or baking sheet. Lash on some tomato sauce, leaving a 1cm border clear around the edge of the pizza, and arrange your favourite toppings.

5 Bake for 15–18 minutes, until golden and crisp. Allow to cool slightly and slice.

MELTED BUTTER, FOR GREASING
250G MACARONI
1 MEDIUM COURGETTE, SLICED DIAGONALLY
EXTRA VIRGIN OLIVE OIL
1 LEEK, SLICED
4 TBSP GRATED PARMESAN
4 TBSP BREADCRUMBS
1 TBSP CHOPPED FRESH PARSLEY, TO GARNISH

FOR THE SAUCE:
50G BUTTER
50G FLOUR
400ML LOW-FAT MILK
350ML CHICKEN STOCK
100G MATURE CHEDDAR CHEESE, GRATED
SALT AND FRESHLY GROUND BLACK PEPPER

1 Preheat the oven to 180°C/fan 160°C/gas 4. Brush a casserole dish with melted butter.

2 Cook the macaroni according to the instructions on the package. Drain and set aside in the pot.

3 Meanwhile, place the courgette slices in a steamer and cook for about 3 minutes, until just tender.

4 To cook the leek, heat some extra virgin olive oil in a medium frying pan over a medium heat. Add the leek slices and sauté for about 5 minutes, until softened but not brown.

5 To make the sauce, place the butter, flour, milk and stock into a large saucepan over a medium heat. Using a whisk, stir continuously until a thick sauce has formed. This should take 7-8 minutes. Stir in the Cheddar cheese and check the seasoning.

6 Mix together the sautéed leeks and some of the courgette slices with the cooked macaroni and the sauce.

7 Pour half of the macaroni cheese into the casserole. Layer with the rest of the courgette slices and pour over another layer of macaroni cheese. Sprinkle over the Parmesan and breadcrumbs.

8 Bake for 20-25 minutes, until the topping is golden. Sprinkle over the chopped parsley and allow to cool slightly before serving.

OUR FAVOURITE MAC AND CHEESE

....

We love this recipe, an old favourite for the younger crowds that come over during the afternoons or at weekends. I like to add some vegetables from our garden patch for freshness – we often have an abundance of courgettes, shallots and leeks, so it's great to be able to use them in this dish.

SERVES 4

350G TAGLIATELLE
EXTRA VIRGIN OLIVE OIL
3 CHICKEN FILLETS, DICED INTO 2CM PIECES
2 MEDIUM ONIONS, THINLY SLICED
ZEST AND JUICE OF ½ LEMON, OR TO TASTE
1 GARLIC CLOVE, CRUSHED
100G FROZEN PEAS
60ML CHICKEN STOCK
6 TBSP CRÈME FRAÎCHE
½ TSP DIJON MUSTARD
SALT AND FRESHLY GROUND BLACK PEPPER
3 TBSP GRATED PARMESAN

TAGLIATELLE WITH CHICKEN AND CREAMY LEMON SAUCE

My mind goes into crazy mode when I realise that the afternoon has gone so quickly and it's almost time to take the children back, so this is my emergency pasta dish. It's quick and it's a crowd pleaser. It's actually faster to make this than it is to get them in the car to go home – there are always a couple hiding!

SERVES 4

1 Cook the tagliatelle according to the instructions on the package. Drain and set aside in the pot.

2 Heat some olive oil in a large saucepan over a medium heat. Add the diced chicken and sauté for 3–4 minutes, until cooked through. Remove from the saucepan with a slotted spoon and set aside on a plate.

3 Add a little more olive oil to the saucepan and raise the heat. Add the onions and lemon zest and sauté for 5–7 minutes, until softened. Add the garlic and cook for 1 minute more. Add in the frozen peas, tossing from time to time, and cook for about 2 minutes.

4 Stir through the chicken stock, crème fraîche, mustard and lemon juice. Return the chicken to the sauce and stir through.

5 Transfer the drained noodles into the creamy sauce, heat through and check the seasoning. Add a little more stock if the sauce is too thick. Sprinkle over the grated Parmesan and serve immediately.

FOR THE FUDGE BROWNIE BARS:
3 EGGS
150G CASTER SUGAR
150G DARK CHOCOLATE, BROKEN INTO PIECES
100G BUTTER
100G SELF-RAISING FLOUR, SIEVED
60G MINI FUDGE PIECES

FOR THE CARAMEL LATTE:
300ML MILK
100ML BOILING WATER
2 TBSP CARAMEL-FLAVOURED SYRUP

1 Preheat the oven to 180°C/fan 160°C/gas 4. Line a 20cm square baking tin with baking parchment.

2 To make the brownie bars, beat the eggs and sugar in a large bowl with a hand whisk until creamy and frothy. Melt the chocolate and butter in a bowl set over a saucepan of simmering water (bain marie) until smooth, taking care not to let the water touch the bottom of the bowl. Stir the melted chocolate into the egg mixture. Add the flour and fudge pieces and stir again. Pour into the baking tin, spreading evenly. Bake for 30–35 minutes, until just set. Leave to cool in the tin for 10 minutes before turning out onto a wire rack. Peel back the parchment from the edges and cut the brownies into thin 3cm bars.

3 To make the lattes, heat the milk in a small pot and add the boiling water. Using a small hand-held milk frother, froth the hot milk. Pour the caramel-flavoured syrup into glasses or mugs. Pour the hot milk into the glasses and serve with the brownie bars.

CARAMEL LATTE WITH FUDGE BROWNIE BARS

....

The girls like to feel special and a little grown up, so I allow them to have a latte – not with coffee, though; the milk is good for them! I also like to serve this at brunch instead of a strong coffee.

MAKES 2 LATTES AND 12–14 BROWNIE BARS

½ TSP GROUND CUMIN

½ TSP GROUND CORIANDER

¼ TSP GARAM MASALA (OPTIONAL)

3 CHICKEN FILLETS, SLICED INTO 2CM STRIPS

SALT AND FRESHLY GROUND BLACK PEPPER

2 TBSP RAPESEED OIL, PLUS EXTRA FOR BRUSHING THE
TORTILLAS

1 RED PEPPER, DESEEDED AND THINLY SLICED

50G MUSHROOMS, SLICED

1 X 400G TIN CHOPPED TOMATOES

1 TBSP CHOPPED FRESH PARSLEY, PLUS EXTRA TO
GARNISH

6 LARGE TORTILLAS

TORTILLA STACK

....

*I let the children get the
tortillas into the oven for
heating and then they can
assemble this one themselves.
It gives them a chance to
develop some good old team
spirit as well as help others.
Of course, when the girls are
calmly cooking, the lads come
into the kitchen and all 'team
spirit' or togetherness flies out
the window! Once the children
put together a tortilla stack of
12 layers – admittedly, it was
for a party, but slicing it was a
bit of a challenge.*

SERVES 4

1 Preheat the oven to 180°C/fan 160°C/gas 4.

2 Mix together the cumin, coriander and garam masala, if using,
in a small bowl. Sprinkle the spice mix over the chicken strips and
season with salt and freshly ground black pepper.

3 Heat the oil in a large frying pan over a medium heat and cook
the chicken strips for about 2 minutes on each side, until golden.
Stir in the sliced red pepper and mushrooms and cook for about
5 minutes, stirring occasionally. Add the chopped tomatoes and
simmer for 3 minutes, until the chicken is cooked though. Add the
chopped parsley and stir.

4 Brush each tortilla with a little oil. Place the tortillas on a piece
of tin foil and wrap them up. Place the foil parcel on a baking tray
in the oven for about 3 minutes to heat them through. Place a
warm tortilla on a platter and spoon some of the chicken mixture
over. Place another tortilla on top and keep layering, ending with
a tortilla. Sprinkle over the chopped parsley and slice into wedges
with a sharp knife.

RASPBERRY
ICE CREAM
SODAS

....

*This is still a very cool treat.
If the children don't like raspberry seeds, then it's best to
sieve the raspberry purée or
try using strawberries instead.
Make a soda bar at birthday
parties for the children to
make the sodas on their own –
it shouldn't be too messy but it
will be a lot of fun.*

SERVES 4

100G RASPBERRIES, PLUS EXTRA TO DECORATE
600ML LEMONADE
SCOOPS OF FROZEN YOGHURT OR ICE CREAM
DRINKING STRAWS

1 Place the raspberries in a food processor and blend until smooth.
Spoon 4–5 tablespoons of the raspberry purée into a tall glass,
pour in the lemonade and float a scoop or two of frozen yoghurt or
ice cream on the top. Add in a straw and a few raspberries on top
to decorate. Serve immediately.

02 } CURRY NIGHT

Friday night is most definitely curry night for me. It's a feast of flavours. Mastering a curry night is easier than you think. Just whip out your spice blender – there's no need to order a takeaway any longer.

There's a great advantage to blending your own spices. Using a good grinder dedicated to spices, you'll be surprised by the beautiful flavours that can be developed. Just remember to heat the dried whole spices in a dry pan for about 30 seconds or so to develop the aroma and then allow to cool slightly before grinding them.

A wonderful Indian lady I've known for years commented that we don't combine our flavours enough these days. My understanding is that to make a memorable meal, it takes about six or seven different dishes. Serve two or more curries at a time, especially a fish or prawn one, a red or green Thai curry, vindaloos or tikkas. And don't forget raitas, fruity pickles and chutneys, fragrant basmati and jasmine rice, piles of poppadoms and some soft, warm naan bread to tear off.

If you feel that the curry sauce is too thick, don't be shy about adding water to loosen the sauce. The sauce should just coat the back of a wooden spoon and the flavours should burst in your mouth, with layers of spiciness.

Now on to the rice. Both basmati and jasmine rice have a unique sweet scent and mild flavour that make the rice easy to serve. They are very versatile and blend with all types of curries. Add flavours like star anise, saffron, coriander leaves or cinnamon to liven up a boring dish.

	ORIGIN	HOW MANY TIMES DO YOU RINSE THE RICE?	COOKING INFO (SERVES 4)
BASMATI	India	Three times in cold water and soak for 10 minutes. Drain.	280g basmati rice to 650ml water. Cook for about 15 minutes. Fluff with a fork.
JASMINE RICE or FRAGRANT or 'STICKY' RICE	Thailand and Vietnam	Only once in cold water. No soaking needed.	280g jasmine rice to 650ml of water. Cook for 10–12 minutes.

ROGAN JOSH PASTE

....

*You won't be able to use all
the curry paste at once, so
keep it sealed in the fridge
for a few weeks and there will
be plenty of opportunities for
dipping into it: spread it on
pork cutlets or thinly over a
beef roast, or even chicken
drumsticks and skewers when
you barbecue. If you feel that
it's a little thick after being in
the fridge, add 1 teaspoon of
sunflower oil to the paste, mix
well and then use as required.*

MAKES ABOUT 100G

2 TSP CUMIN SEEDS
2 TSP CORIANDER SEEDS
1 TSP BLACK PEPPERCORNS
2 RED PEPPERS, ROASTED AND ROUGHLY CHOPPED
2 GARLIC CLOVES, ROUGHLY CHOPPED
1 RED CHILLI, ROUGHLY CHOPPED
1 X 2CM PIECE OF FRESH GINGER, GRATED
SMALL BUNCH OF FRESH CORIANDER, ROUGHLY CHOPPED
2 TBSP VEGETABLE OIL
2 TBSP TOMATO PURÉE
2 TSP GARAM MASALA
2 TSP TURMERIC
1 TSP SMOKED PAPRIKA
½ TSP SALT

1 Heat a small frying pan over a low to medium heat and toast
the cumin, coriander and black peppercorns for 30 seconds to
1 minute, until fragrant. Allow to cool.

2 Place all the other ingredients into a blender or pestle and
mortar. Add the cool, toasted spices and blend into a smooth
paste. This will keep sealed in the fridge for 2 to 3 weeks.

ROGAN JOSH CURRY
....

*This is the low and slow curry
– a warm, comforting dish that
won't make you feel too hot. I
never want my friends to feel
uncomfortable or red faced
or have to mop their brow!
The joy of cooking curries is
that you can add as much
or as little spice as you wish
and you can tone it down
with an aubergine lentil dhal
(page 21). For years, I always
thought of dhals as boring or
even bland, but they play an
important role in a curry night
by cooling things down.*

SERVES 4-6

3 TBSP VEGETABLE OIL

2 ONIONS, FINELY CHOPPED

2 GARLIC CLOVES, CRUSHED

1 X 2CM PIECE OF FRESH GINGER, GRATED

2 TBSP HOMEMADE ROGAN JOSH PASTE (PAGE 14)

700G LEG OF LAMB, TRIMMED AND DICED INTO 3CM
  PIECES

400G TOMATOES, DICED

250ML WATER

125ML NATURAL YOGHURT

SALT

HANDFUL OF FRESH CORIANDER, CHOPPED

1 Heat the oil in a large saucepan over a medium heat. Add the
onions and cook for 4-5 minutes, until softened. Add the garlic,
ginger and rogan josh paste and cook for 1 minute more, stirring all
the time.

2 Add the lamb pieces and fry for 3-4 minutes, until golden brown
on all sides. Stir in the tomatoes, water, natural yoghurt and salt to
taste (about $1/2$ teaspoon should be right).

3 Bring the curry to the boil, stirring from time to time. Reduce
the heat to low, cover with a lid and simmer for about 1 hour 45
minutes, or until the sauce has thickened and the lamb is tender.
You may need to add a little water from time to time if the sauce is
too thick. Garnish with chopped fresh corriander.

PANEER TIKKA MASALA

....

When it's raining and you don't fancy cleaning your cupboards again, why not try making your own paneer? It's so easy. You'll need 1.125 litres of full-fat milk and ½ teaspoon lemon juice. Heat 125ml of the milk in a small saucepan. When it's warm, add the lemon juice. Pour the remaining 1 litre of milk into a separate medium saucepan and bring to the boil. When the milk begins to boil, add the lemon milk and reduce the heat, stirring continually until the milk has completely curdled. Remove from the heat and strain the curds through a piece of muslin. Hold it under running water for a minute and then squeeze out the excess water. Hang the paneer over a bowl for 20 minutes to drain. Tie up the muslin and then place it under a heavy object for 2 hours, after which time it can be sliced into pieces.

SERVES 4

150G PANEER, DICED INTO 2CM PIECES

3 TBSP TIKKA MASALA PASTE

BUTTER OR GHEE

2 ONIONS, SLICED

½ TSP SALT

1 X 400G TIN CHOPPED TOMATOES

1 TBSP TOMATO PURÉE

100ML WATER

200G COOKED BLACK BEANS

4 TBSP NATURAL YOGHURT

MINT LEAVES, TO SERVE

SAFFRON CINNAMON BASMATI RICE (PAGE 24), TO SERVE

1 Preheat the grill.

2 Toss the paneer in 1 tablespoon of the tikka masala paste and place on a non stick-baking tray. Put the paneer under the grill, turning from time to time and keeping an eye on it so that it doesn't burn. Once it's golden, remove from the grill and set aside.

3 Heat a little butter or ghee in a medium saucepan over a medium heat and add the onions and salt. Sauté for 8–10 minutes, until golden and softened. Add the rest of the tikka masala paste and cook for about 4 minutes, then stir in the chopped tomatoes, the tomato purée and the water. Cook for a further 3 minutes.

4 Stir in the cooked black beans and natural yoghurt and simmer very gently for 5 minutes. Add the paneer to the sauce and simmer for a further 2 minutes. Check the seasoning, adding a little salt if required. Sprinkle over the mint leaves and serve with saffron cinnamon basmati rice.

2 TBSP VEGETABLE OIL

½ TSP FENUGREEK SEEDS

1 SMALL RED ONION, FINELY CHOPPED

1 GREEN CHILLI, WHOLE BUT PIERCED 2 OR 3 TIMES

1 X 4CM PIECE OF FRESH GINGER, HALF PEELED AND
   JULIENNED AND HALF GRATED

3 SMALL TOMATOES, ROUGHLY CHOPPED

3 GARLIC CLOVES

1 TSP GROUND CUMIN

1 TSP GROUND CORIANDER

¾ TSP GARAM MASALA

¼ TSP TURMERIC

SALT

400G LARGE RAW PRAWNS, SHELLED, DEVEINED
   AND RINSED

4 TBSP DOUBLE CREAM

JUICE OF ½ LEMON

1 TBSP ROUGHLY CHOPPED FRESH CORIANDER LEAVES,
   TO GARNISH

NAAN BREAD OR POPPADOMS, TO SERVE

NORTH INDIAN PRAWN CURRY

1 Heat the oil in a large non-stick saucepan over a medium heat. Add the fenugreek seeds and heat for about 30 seconds to release the aromatics. Add a little more oil to the fenugreek seeds and stir in the red onion, green chilli and the sliced ginger. Gently cook for about 5 minutes, until the onions are just softened.

2 Place the tomatoes, garlic and the grated ginger into a food processor and blend to a fine purée. Stir this purée into the onions along with the ground cumin, ground coriander, garam masala and turmeric and season with a little salt. Cook over a medium-low heat for 8-10 minutes, stirring from time to time, until it thickens.

3 Add the prawns and enough water to cover them by half. Increase the heat and bring to the boil, then reduce the heat and simmer gently for about 3 minutes, or until the prawns are cooked. The sauce should be light but not watery. Turn off the heat and stir in the cream. Add half the lemon juice and then taste the sauce, adjusting the seasoning and adding more lemon juice if necessary. Sprinkle over the chopped coriander and serve with naan bread or poppadoms.

This curry doesn't take much effort to make. The prawns sit proudly in the superb tangy cream sauce with ginger undertones. Northern India's cuisine has more yoghurt, cream and butter, and because the climate is very hot during the day and cooler at night, it has fabulous fruits and nuts, so chopped fresh fruits like figs or mango would often be served with the meal.

SERVES 4

FOR THE PASTE:
3 RED CHILLIES, TRIMMED AND LEFT WHOLE
2 SHALLOTS, ROUGHLY CHOPPED
2 GARLIC CLOVES
1 LEMONGRASS STALK, ROUGHLY CHOPPED
1 X 3CM PIECE OF FRESH GINGER, GRATED
ZEST OF 1 LIME
3 TBSP ROUGHLY CHOPPED FRESH CORIANDER
1 TBSP VEGETABLE OIL

FOR THE CURRY:
3 TBSP VEGETABLE OIL
1½ RED CHILLIES, DESEEDED AND FINELY SLICED
1 MEDIUM COURGETTE, ROUGHLY DICED
1 YELLOW PEPPER, DESEEDED AND CUT INTO 2CM DICE
150G GREEN BEANS, SLICED LENGTHWAYS
100G CHESTNUT MUSHROOMS, HALVED
2 TBSP SOY SAUCE
1 TSP DARK BROWN SUGAR
400ML LOW-FAT COCONUT MILK
JUICE OF ½ LIME
NAM PLA (FISH SAUCE), TO SEASON
JASMINE RICE (SEE PAGE 13), TO SERVE

FRAGRANT THAI RED VEGETABLE CURRY

....

A great favourite in our home, this is quick and tasty and is also a convenient midweek meal served with brown jasmine rice. Add strips of chicken fillets or even prawns to this one and everyone will think that you are the best! The paste will also keep in the fridge for about 10 days.

SERVES 4

1 Place all the ingredients for the paste in a food processor and blend.

2 Using a large wok or frying pan, heat the oil over a medium heat. Add 2 tablespoons of the paste and fry for about 2 minutes, stirring from time to time. Add one-third of the sliced chilli and all the courgette to the pan and cook for about 3 minutes. Add the yellow pepper and stir-fry for about 2 minutes. Toss in the green beans and cook for 1 minute, then add the mushrooms, soy sauce and brown sugar. Cook for about 2 minutes.

3 Carefully stir in the coconut milk and reduce the heat to a simmer for about 3 minutes. Add the lime juice to taste and check the seasoning, adding dashes of nam pla as necessary.

4 Garnish with the rest of the sliced red chillies and serve immediately with jasmine rice.

200G RED LENTILS, RINSED

500ML WATER

½ TSP TURMERIC

½ TSP SALT

VEGETABLE OIL

2 ONIONS, THINLY SLICED

2 GARLIC CLOVES, CRUSHED

1 X 3CM PIECE OF FRESH GINGER, GRATED

4 CURRY LEAVES, CHOPPED FINELY

1 TSP GARAM MASALA

1 SMALL AUBERGINE, THINLY SLICED

1 Place the lentils, water and turmeric in a medium saucepan and bring to the boil. Reduce the heat and simmer for 15 minutes, or until soft. Stir in the salt.

2 Meanwhile, heat a little vegetable oil in a large frying pan over a medium heat. Add the onions and sauté for 7–8 minutes, until softened but not brown. Stir in the garlic and ginger and cook for a further 2 minutes. Add the curry leaves and garam masala and cook for 2 minutes more. Pour the lentils into the frying pan with the onions and gently simmer over a low heat for 8 minutes.

3 Heat a large frying pan with a little vegetable oil over a medium heat. Add a few slices of aubergine at a time and fry for 2 minutes on each side, or until crispy and cooked. Drain on kitchen paper and keep warm.

4 To serve, spoon the dhal into a warm serving bowl and arrange the aubergine slices on top.

AUBERGINE LENTIL DHAL

. . . .

Dhals are great way to cool down the whole curry experience. I just had to add an Italian influence here by adding the aubergines on top. You could dice them and stir them into the dhal as well.

SERVES 4

CHEF DHEERAJ'S MONKFISH AND AUBERGINE CURRY

·············

A traditional mild Mauritian fish curry served with home-made parathas, this recipe comes from my friend Dheeraj Ramgoolam, head chef at the Druids Glen Resort. When he prepared it at the Some Like It Hot cookery class here at our school, we all couldn't stop eating it. Thanks, Dheeraj, this is a hottie (not literally!). It has become one of my favourites.

SERVES 4

FOR THE CURRY POWDER:

2 TBSP GROUND CORIANDER

1 TBSP GROUND CUMIN

1 TSP GROUND TURMERIC

½ TSP RED CHILLI POWDER (OR MORE, ACCORDING TO TASTE)

½ TSP CARDAMOM SEEDS

½ TSP GROUND CLOVES OR 3 WHOLE CLOVES, GROUND IN A PESTLE AND MORTAR

½ TSP GROUND CINNAMON

¼ TSP FENNEL SEEDS

½ TSP GROUND GINGER

½ TSP GARLIC POWDER

FOR THE MONKFISH AND AUBERGINE CURRY:

VEGETABLE OIL, FOR FRYING

3 MEDIUM GARLIC CLOVES, CHOPPED

1 LARGE ONION, FINELY SLICED

4 MEDIUM TOMATOES, PEELED AND CHOPPED

1 TSP FENUGREEK SEEDS

250ML CHICKEN STOCK

400G FRESH MONKFISH TAIL, WASHED AND SLICED ABOUT 2½ CM THICK

JUICE OF 1 LEMON

PINCH OF TURMERIC

SALT AND FRESHLY GROUND BLACK PEPPER

1 LARGE AUBERGINE, DICED INTO 1CM PIECES

SALT AND FRESHLY GROUND BLACK PEPPER

SMALL BUNCH OF FRESH CORIANDER LEAVES, CHOPPED, TO GARNISH

PARATHAS (PAGE 23), TO SERVE

1 To make the curry powder, heat a large dry frying pan over a medium heat. Add all the curry powder ingredients except for the ground ginger and garlic powder and gently heat for 30 seconds. Cool slightly, then combine all the toasted spices in a blender or food processor. Add in the ground ginger and garlic powder and process to a fine powder. (This will keep for 2 weeks in an airtight container.)

2 To make the curry, heat 4 tablespoons of vegetable oil in a large, deep saucepan over a medium heat. Add the garlic and onion and reduce the heat. Sauté for 5–6 minutes, until lightly golden brown.

3 Add the curry powder and cook on a low heat for about 2 minutes, until the oil separates out. Add the chopped tomatoes and fenugreek seeds and cook for about 10 minutes. Stir in the chicken stock and bring to the boil, then reduce the heat and gently simmer for 25 minutes.

4 Meanwhile, marinate the fish with the lemon juice, a pinch of turmeric and a pinch of salt and pepper for 10 minutes prior to cooking. Heat a medium frying pan with vegetable oil over a medium-high heat and shallow fry the fish pieces for about 5 minutes, until cooked. Drain on kitchen paper and set aside.

5 Heat 2cm of vegetable oil in a deep frying pan over a medium heat and fry the aubergine for about 4 minutes, until golden. Drain on kitchen paper and set aside.

6 Add the cooked fish and aubergine to the sauce and cook for a further 5 minutes, until heated through. Garnish the fish curry with the chopped fresh coriander and serve with mini parathas.

PARATHAS

100G PLAIN FLOUR

1 TSP GHEE OR CLARIFIED BUTTER, PLUS EXTRA FOR BRUSHING

1 TSP OIL, PLUS EXTRA FOR RUBBING OVER THE DOUGH

¼ TSP SALT

MAKES 16 SMALL TRIANGLES

1 Mix together the flour, ghee or clarified butter, oil, salt and enough water to make a soft dough. Rub oil over the dough, wrap it tightly in parchment paper and leave to rest for 1 hour.

2 Tear off a piece of dough about the size of a golf ball. Using a rolling pin, roll it into a small, thin circle on a floured surface. Spread the dough with a little ghee or clarified butter. Fold in half again and spread a little more clarified butter or ghee over. Roll into a circle again, ensuring it's very thin. Slice the circle into quarters to form triangular wedges.

3 Heat a large, dry, flat, non-stick pan over a medium heat. Place the paratha triangles in the pan and cook for about 1 minute on each side, until light golden brown. Serve with a curry.

SAFFRON CINNAMON BASMATI RICE

·····································

Add a good pinch of turmeric to the rice for a warm sparkle. Another way of serving rice with a curry is to make rice cakes: add 1 beaten egg and 1 tablespoon chopped fresh coriander to about 250g cooked rice and shape into a small rice cake. Heat 2 tablespoons of sunflower oil in a large frying pan over a medium heat and cook for 2 minutes on each side. Keep warm and serve with a creamy chicken korma.

SERVES 4

280G BASMATI RICE
650ML COLD WATER
4 STRANDS OF SAFFRON, SOAKED IN 3 TBSP WATER
1 CINNAMON STICK, BRUISED
PINCH OF SALT

1 Rinse the rice three times in cold water, then soak for 10 minutes and drain.

2 Place the rice and water into a medium saucepan. Add the saffron and its soaking water and the cinnamon stick.

3 Cover the pan with a lid. Bring to the boil, then reduce to a low heat and cook for 8-10 minutes. Check a grain of rice for doneness. When it's ready, remove the cinnamon stick. Fluff up the rice with a fork and season with a little salt.

280G BASMATI RICE

7 WHOLE BLACK PEPPERCORNS

2 CARDAMOM PODS, PODS CRUSHED AND SEEDS REMOVED

1 TSP CUMIN SEEDS

VEGETABLE OIL

2 ONIONS, SLICED

2 GARLIC CLOVES, FINELY CHOPPED

650ML COLD WATER

ZEST AND JUICE OF ½ LEMON

4 TBSP CASHEW NUTS, TOASTED

SALT

GOOD HANDFUL OF CORIANDER, ROUGHLY CHOPPED

1 Soak the rice in cold water for 10 minutes.

2 Place the peppercorns, cardamom seeds and cumin seeds in a pestle and mortar and grind until smooth. Heat a non-stick frying pan over a medium-low heat and add the spices. Cook for 1 minute, or until the aromas are released.

3 Heat a little vegetable oil in a saucepan over a medium heat and add the onions. Reduce the heat to low and sauté the onions for 8 minutes, until golden. Add the garlic and the cooked spices to the saucepan and cook for 2 minutes.

4 Drain the rice and add to the saucepan with the water. Bring to the boil, then reduce the heat to low, cover with a lid and cook for about 15 minutes, until the rice is tender and all the liquid has been absorbed. Check a grain of rice – if it's not tender, cook for a further 3-4 minutes. Fluff up the rice with a fork and stir in the lemon zest and juice as well as the cashew nuts. Check the seasoning, adding salt if required.

5 Sprinkle over the chopped coriander and serve immediately with a rogan josh curry (page 16).

CASHEW PILAU RICE WITH CORIANDER

....

You can change this from a side dish to a main course by adding a few seared chicken thighs, one more onion and a few chopped green beans to the pilau rice. Bake in the oven for 35–40 minutes for a delicious snack.

SERVES 4

CHILLI BHAJIS WITH SPICY APRICOT PICKLE AND COCONUT RAITA

....

Bhajis are my favourite and no curry night is complete without them! Team them with a good fruit chutney or pickle to offset your fabulous meal. You can make the batter the day before, leave it in the fridge and just add 1 table-spoon of gram (chickpea) flour into the mixture before you fry them off for serving. Gram flour is available from health food shops and some supermarkets.

SERVES 4

FOR THE BHAJIS:
2 TSP CORIANDER SEEDS
1 TSP CUMIN SEEDS
100G GRAM (CHICKPEA) FLOUR
½ TSP BAKING POWDER
½ TSP SALT
1 LARGE ONION, VERY FINELY CHOPPED
ABOUT 40ML VEGETABLE OIL

FOR THE APRICOT PICKLE:
100G LIGHT BROWN SUGAR
180ML WATER
175ML WHITE WINE VINEGAR
1 TSP GROUND CUMIN
½ TSP GROUND CORIANDER
½ TSP MUSTARD SEEDS, GROUND
350G READY-TO-EAT DRIED APRICOTS, ROUGHLY CHOPPED
1 BAY LEAF
60G RAISINS
SALT

FOR THE COCONUT RAITA:
VEGETABLE OIL
½ ONION, SLICED
½ TSP CORIANDER SEEDS
½ TSP MUSTARD SEEDS
100ML NATURAL YOGHURT
2 TBSP GRATED COCONUT
2 TBSP RAISINS
2 TBSP CASHEWS, TOASTED AND ROUGHLY CHOPPED
3 MINT LEAVES, FINELY CHOPPED
2 TBSP COCONUT FLAKES, TOASTED, TO GARNISH

1 To make the bhajis, lightly toast the coriander seeds and cumin seeds in a hot dry pan for 30 seconds and set aside.

2 Sieve the flour into a bowl and add the toasted seeds, baking powder, salt and finely chopped onion. Add just enough water to make a thick batter. Heat about 40ml of vegetable oil in a deep frying pan over a high heat. Drop small spoonfuls of batter into the hot oil in batches. Fry for about 3 minutes, turning once, until golden on both sides. Drain on kitchen paper and keep warm until ready to serve.

3 To prepare the apricot pickle, combine the brown sugar, water, vinegar, cumin, coriander and ground mustard in a medium saucepan over a medium-high heat and bring to the boil. Reduce the heat and simmer for 5 minutes, then add the apricots and bay leaf and simmer for about 15 minutes, until soft. Add the raisins and cook very gently for 25–30 minutes, stirring from time to time. Add a little water if the pickle is drying out. Check the seasoning, adding a little salt if necessary. Remove the bay leaf.

4 To make the raita, heat a frying pan with a little vegetable oil over a medium heat. Add the sliced onion and sauté for 6 minutes, until soft and golden. Meanwhile, crush the coriander and mustard seeds in a pestle and mortar. Add the crushed seeds to the onion and cook for 2 minutes. Set aside to cool.

5 Mix together the yoghurt, grated coconut, raisins, toasted cashews and mint leaves and add the cooled onions. Mix well, then garnish with the toasted coconut flakes and set aside.

6 Serve the bhajis, apricot pickle and raita in small bowls for everyone to help themselves.

1 X 397G TIN CONDENSED MILK
1 SMALL MANGO, PEELED AND DICED SMALL
ZEST AND JUICE OF 1 LIME
300ML DOUBLE CREAM, LIGHTLY WHIPPED
3 TBSP PISTACHIOS, ROUGHLY CHOPPED

FOR THE MANGO SYRUP:
100G CASTER SUGAR
100ML WATER
1 MEDIUM MANGO, PEELED AND DICED SMALL
ZEST OF 1 LIME

1 Line 8 dariole moulds or ramekins with plastic wrap and place on a tray in the freezer.

2 Pour the condensed milk into a large bowl. Add the diced mango and the lime zest and juice. Stir well. Fold the lightly whipped double cream into the condensed milk and mango mixture. Ladle into the moulds or ramekins and freeze initially for 30 minutes, then cover with plastic wrap and freeze for a further 5 hours or overnight.

3 Meanwhile, to make the mango syrup, pour the sugar and water into a small saucepan and bring to the boil. Reduce the heat and simmer for 5–6 minutes, until a syrup has formed. Add the diced mango and lime zest to the syrup and remove from the heat to cool.

4 To unmould and serve, dip the moulds or ramekins in hot water for a few seconds, then turn them upside down and slide out onto a serving plate. Sprinkle pistachios on top and spoon over some mango syrup. Serve immediately.

MANGO KULFI WITH PISTACHIOS

....

A traditional kulfi is made with milk and sugar boiled for a very long time, but adding the condensed milk makes it a much easier process and very delicious. It's so quick: scoop it into mini cones and serve it as a late night treat or serve it in Indian tea glasses and drizzle over the mango syrup.

SERVES 8

CHAPTER

03 { MOVIE NIGHT

....

Movie night is my time to kick my shoes off and relax. My dream is to have an outdoor movie night. I can imagine soft cushions on a patio, a warm, balmy evening, deliciously elegant cocktails and lanterns in the trees – and then I have to bring myself back down to earth and remind myself that knowing my luck, I would get gently nibbled by overzealous midges, as usual!

So back to the indoor movie night. What could be better than curling up on a soft, comfy sofa with a good movie for a romantic movie night in, or inviting some friends over and going all out with surprises for them? There are some great combos for popcorn that I love: cinnamon, honey and apple come to mind, or cumin and dried mango, lemon salt, or cranberry and salted caramel. Serve herb potato wedges wrapped in newspaper or have a vintage sweets tray with bags of old-fashioned sweets and chocolate bars to serve with coffee.

The important point here is to be organised. Serve easy-to-eat finger foods and have everything ready so that you too can enjoy the movie. Make sure that you have loads of napkins and side plates and have the drinks on tap.

RAPESEED OIL

8 LARGE TORTILLAS

4 TBSP SPICY MANGO CHUTNEY

8 SLICES ROAST CHICKEN

4 TBSP COOKED BLACK BEANS, MASHED SLIGHTLY

2 ROASTED RED PEPPERS (FROM A JAR IS FINE), SLICED
  INTO STRIPS

120G MATURE CHEDDAR, GRATED

SALT AND FRESHLY GROUND BLACK PEPPER

GOOD HANDFUL OF FRESH CORIANDER, ROUGHLY
  CHOPPED, TO GARNISH

CHICKEN AND BEAN QUESADILLAS

The trick here is to use a good melting cheese to hold all your favourite ingredients together. Chop the quesadillas up and stack them on a wooden board. They aren't too messy, so they're great finger food. You can even make a sweet quesdailla with chocolate spread, thin plum wedges and some crunchy chopped walnuts.

SERVES 4

1 Heat a little oil in a large frying pan over a medium heat. Place 1 tortilla in the pan and spread 1 tablespoon of chutney over. Top with 2 slices of roast chicken, 1 tablespoon of mashed black beans and one-quarter of the red pepper strips and sprinkle over some cheese. Season with salt and freshly ground black pepper. Press another tortilla down on top of the filling and cook in the frying pan for $1\frac{1}{2}$–2 minutes, or until the bottom tortilla starts to turn golden, before flipping it over and cooking on the other side until golden. Repeat with the remaining tortillas.

2 Slice the quesadillas into neat triangles. Pile on a board, sprinkle over the coriander and serve immediately.

FOR THE PASTRY:

250G PLAIN FLOUR

125G BUTTER, CHILLED
AND DICED

1 EGG

1 EGG YOLK

FOR THE FILLING:

EXTRA VIRGIN OLIVE OIL

4 SHALLOTS, TRIMMED AND
CHOPPED INTO WEDGES

1 LEEK, RINSED AND FINELY
SLICED

1 TSP GROUND CUMIN

150G ROAST CHICKEN,
DICED INTO 2CM PIECES

100G SOFT GOAT'S CHEESE

50G SPINACH, WASHED AND
ROUGHLY CHOPPED

ZEST AND JUICE OF
½ LEMON

4 TBSP CREAM

SALT AND FRESHLY GROUND
BLACK PEPPER

1 EGG, BEATEN

LEEK AND CHICKEN FREEFORM PIES

··········

*These are probably one of my
favourite casual foods and
my friends always ask for the
recipe. If time is on your side,
try preparing mini versions to
serve at drinks parties. Don't
be too worried if the pastry
is a little crumbly – patch it
together as you go; it's a rustic
pie. The pastry is rich and just
melts with the chicken filling.
Try adding diced roasted
butternut squash to the pies
instead of the chicken or even
diced Irish black pudding.*

SERVES 4

1 To make the pastry, sieve the flour into a medium bowl. Use your
fingertips to rub in the butter until the mix resembles fine breadcrumbs. Using a knife, blend the egg and egg yolk into the mix to
form a soft pastry. Turn out the pastry onto a lightly floured surface
and shape into a ball. Wrap in parchment paper or plastic wrap and
place in the fridge for about 30 minutes to rest.

2 Meanwhile, to make the filling, heat some extra virgin olive oil in
a large frying pan over a medium heat. Add the shallots and leek
and sauté for about 6 minutes, until soft but not brown. Stir in the
cumin and sauté for 2 minutes more. Allow to cool slightly.

3 Combine the shallots, leek, roast chicken, goat's cheese, spinach,
lemon zest and juice and the cream in a medium bowl. Season with
salt and freshly ground black pepper.

4 Preheat the oven to 200°C/fan 180°C/gas 6. Line a large baking
tray with parchment paper.

5 Turn the pastry onto a lightly floured surface and divide into
4 portions. Roll each portion into a 15cm disc (a side plate is a
good template) about 3mm thick. Spoon about one-quarter of the
filling into the centre of each pastry disc. Fold in the edge of each
pastry disc to partially enclose the filling, leaving the centre of the
pies open. Press the pastry edges down and carefully transfer to
the lined baking tray. Brush the pastry with a little beaten egg.

6 Bake for about 20 minutes, or until the pastry is golden and
cooked through. Allow the pies to cool for 5 minutes before
serving.

3 MEDIUM SWEET POTATOES, PEELED AND CUT INTO
   WEDGES
50G BUTTER, MELTED
ZEST OF 1 LEMON
¾ TSP GROUND CUMIN
¾ TSP SEA SALT
½ TSP BLACK PEPPER
¼ TSP GROUND CORIANDER

1 Preheat the oven to 200°C/fan 180°C/gas 6.

2 Toss the sweet potatoes in the melted butter, lemon zest and
spices. Transfer onto a baking tray and roast for 20–25 minutes,
until they're tender and golden. Season to taste and allow to cool
slightly before serving.

LEMON CUMIN SWEET POTATO WEDGES

....

*Try these with parsnips as well
as apples and carrots. They
all make fabulous homemade
crisps! A mandolin works well
for making very thin crisps,
but these are wedges so that
you can serve them in paper
cones. Looks interesting and
no washing up!*

SERVES 4

SUNFLOWER OIL
100G DICED PANCETTA
200G POPPING CORN
MAPLE SYRUP, TO DRIZZLE
ZEST OF 1 LIME
PINCH OF SEA SALT

1 Heat a large saucepan with a little sunflower oil over a high
heat. Add the diced pancetta and sauté until crispy. Remove the
pancetta with a slotted spoon. Drain on kitchen paper and set
aside.

2 Reduce the heat to medium and add a little more oil to the
pot. Add the popping corn and put on the lid. Cook for 1 minute,
shaking the saucepan occasionally, until the popping stops – don't
remove the lid before then!

3 Tip the popcorn into a large bowl. Add the crispy pancetta
pieces, a good drizzle of maple syrup, the lime zest and a pinch of
sea salt. Toss together and add more salt or syrup, to taste.

PANCETTA AND MAPLE POPCORN

....

*This is so tasty, you'll need
to make more … and more!
There are many flavours to
experiment with, but pancetta
and maple is a classic and
everyone will love it. Popcorn
flavours can be trial and
error, so you may need to add
a little more salt or maple
syrup. Begin with just a little
flavouring, as you can't take
out the salt or syrup if you've
added too much!*

SERVES 4

FARMER'S HOT DOG WITH CORN RELISH

....

I have to include something from the farm – there are good-quality artisan sausage makers here and there's nothing nicer than a good old hot dog. Forget about those processed things! A good bread roll is essential to go with the relish. On a rainy day when the children want something to do, you could even prepare your own rolls using pizza dough (page 4). Shape the dough into rolls and allow to rise in a warm place. Brush with a little olive oil, sprinkle over some poppy seeds and bake in a hot oven (about 200°C/fan 180°C/gas 6) for approximately 20 minutes, depending on the size.

MAKES 4

RAPESEED OIL
4 GOOD-QUALITY BUTCHER SAUSAGES
4 GOOD-QUALITY BREAD ROLLS, SLICED
TOMATO KETCHUP, TO SERVE
FRESH CORIANDER SPRIGS, TO GARNISH

FOR THE CORN RELISH:
RAPESEED OIL
1 RED ONION, THINLY SLICED
1 RED PEPPER, ROUGHLY CHOPPED
1 RED CHILLI, FINELY CHOPPED
¼ TSP PAPRIKA
100G SWEETCORN
SALT AND FRESHLY GROUND BLACK PEPPER

1 To make the relish, heat a medium saucepan with a little rapeseed oil. Add the sliced onion and sauté for about 5 minutes, until softened but not brown, stirring from time to time. Add the red pepper and red chilli together with the paprika and cook for 3-4 minutes, stirring from time to time. Stir in the sweetcorn and cook for 2-3 minutes. Add salt and freshly ground black pepper to season and cook for a further 2 minutes. Set aside to cool.

2 In the meantime, heat a little rapeseed oil in a large frying pan over a medium heat. Add the sausages and carefully cook until golden on all sides and cooked through. Set aside.

3 To assemble, place the bread rolls on a serving platter, spoon over a little tomato ketchup and place the sausages in the centre, then spoon over the corn relish and place coriander sprigs on top.

2 TBSP SUNFLOWER OIL

3 CHICKEN BREASTS, TRIMMED AND SLICED

1 TSP GROUND CUMIN

1 ONION, FINELY CHOPPED

1 RED CHILLI, FINELY CHOPPED

1 GARLIC CLOVE, FINELY CHOPPED

300G TINNED KIDNEY BEANS, DRAINED

4 LARGE OR 8 SMALL CORN TACOS, WARMED

1 TBSP CHOPPED FRESH PARSLEY, TO GARNISH

2 TBSP CREAM CHEESE, TO SERVE

FOR THE LIME AND AVOCADO SALSA:

2 TOMATOES, DESEEDED AND DICED

1 RIPE AVOCADO, DICED

1 MILD CHILLI, DESEEDED AND FINELY SLICED

1 SMALL BUNCH FRESH CORIANDER, CHOPPED

ZEST AND JUICE OF 1 LIME

SALT AND FRESHLY GROUND BLACK PEPPER

SPICY CHICKEN TACOS WITH LIME AND AVOCADO SALSA

....

Guests can assemble these. The chicken, bean and onion mix can be made ahead of time. Wrap them in funky napkins, as they do tend to be messy, and serve in a basket – less tidying up for you to do!

MAKES 4 LARGE OR 8 SMALL TACOS

1 To make the salsa, combine all the ingredients in a bowl and mix together.

2 Preheat the oven to 180°C/fan 160°C/gas 4.

3 Heat the oil in a saucepan over a medium heat. Sauté the chicken slices with the cumin for 3 minutes, until cooked through and lightly browned. Using a slotted spoon, remove the chicken from the pan. Add the onion to the pan and sauté for about 5 minutes. Add the chilli and garlic and cook for a further 2 minutes. Add the kidney beans and return the chicken to the pan and cook for 4-5 minutes, until fully heated through.

4 Place the tacos on a baking tray and heat in the oven for 2 minutes, until warm. Spoon the chicken filling into the tacos and return to the oven for about 2 minutes.

5 Sprinkle with parsley, spoon over a little cream cheese and serve with the lime and avocado salsa.

FOR THE BASE:
250G PLAIN DIGESTIVE BISCUITS
160G BUTTER, MELTED

FOR THE CHEESECAKE:
100G DARK CHOCOLATE
300G CREAM CHEESE
100G ICING SUGAR, SIEVED
250ML CREAM, WHIPPED
2 TBSP ESPRESSO COFFEE
CHOCOLATE SHAVINGS, TO DECORATE

1 To prepare the base, line a 23cm springform tin with parchment paper and brush the sides with a little of the melted butter.

2 Place the biscuits into a food processor and whizz until fairly smooth. Pour into a large bowl and add most of the melted butter, until the crumbs hold together when pressed, adding more of the butter if needed. Spoon the biscuit crumbs into the base of the tin and press down. Place in the fridge to set for about 30 minutes.

3 To prepare the filling, melt the chocolate in a bowl set over a saucepan of simmering water (bain marie) until smooth, taking care not to let the water touch the bottom of the bowl. Allow to cool slightly.

4 Spoon the cream cheese into a large bowl. Fold in the icing sugar and whipped cream and add the espresso coffee. Carefully fold in the melted chocolate just so that it forms a marbled effect.

5 Remove the biscuit base from the fridge and pour in the chocolate cream cheese mix, smoothing the top. Chill in the fridge for at least 6 hours, or preferably overnight.

6 To serve, carefully slide a knife around the edge of the cheesecake and unclip the tin. Using a palette knife, slide the cheesecake onto a cake stand or plate. Arrange the chocolate shavings on top and slice to serve.

COFFEE CHEESECAKE

....

This cheesecake is smooth, mousse-like and fairly light, not like a heavy baked one. Serve with a good cup of coffee or a glass of amaretto on ice.

SERVES 8-10

CHAPTER
04

LATE LATE NIGHT
SUPPER

We deserve an easy treat after a long day. Now is the time to enjoy an evening out and indulge in something sweet, a few more carbs, gooey, stringy cheese melts or scrumptious pastas. If you want something quick, try the Mussels with Saffron and Cream on page 92.

I don't know what it is, but I'm always starving after coming back from a show or concert. I want to rustle up something that's fast, simple and made from ingredients that I have in the fridge and pantry and that I don't have to think too much about at that hour either.

There are a few ingredients that I like to keep on hand no matter what time of the year – or night – it is so that I can whip up a late night supper: a jar or two of artichoke hearts, a few jars of roasted red and yellow peppers, a good pesto, pine nuts and a few tins of quality Italian chopped tomatoes, plus pancetta and a good-quality local artisan Cheddar in the fridge. Oh, and a few packets of pasta, of course!

ROAST MED VEG PASTA

100G CHERRY TOMATOES

12 ASPARAGUS SPEARS, TRIMMED AND CUT INTO
   QUARTERS

3 GARLIC CLOVES, SLICED

1 RED PEPPER, DICED

1 SMALL AUBERGINE, DICED

2 TBSP EXTRA VIRGIN OLIVE OIL

4 SMALL ROSEMARY SPRIGS

400G FUSILLI

2 TBSP BASIL PESTO

Parmesan shavings, to garnish

1 Preheat the oven to 190°C/fan 170°C/gas 5.

2 Place the cherry tomatoes, asparagus spears, garlic, red pepper and aubergine in a roasting pan. Drizzle with the extra virgin olive oil and tuck in the rosemary sprigs. Roast for 20–25 minutes, until the vegetables are golden and tender.

3 Meanwhile, bring a large pot of salted water to the boil. Cook the fusilli according to the packet instructions. Before draining, reserve 4 tablespoons of the cooking liquid.

4 Spoon the roasted vegetables and their juices into a serving bowl. Add the warm fusilli pasta and stir in the pesto together with 3 tablespoons of the pasta cooking liquid. If you feel that more liquid is required, add another tablespoon of the cooking water. Sprinkle over the Parmesan shavings and serve immediately.

This recipe is pretty quick. The roasted vegetables could be prepared ahead of time and having some readily available in your fridge is a good plan. Or if you have a group of friends over, get everyone involved in helping you and there will be much laughter: one on drinks, one on chopping, one on cooking the pasta, one on timing and there you are – you can sit back and relax! You could also add spinach to the warm vegetables before adding in the pasta and grate a little nutmeg over. Fusilli pasta is great to use here, as the sauce coats the twisted pasta.

SERVES 4

350G PORK FILLET, SLICED INTO THIN STRIPS
(ASK YOUR BUTCHER TO DO THIS)

3 TBSP OYSTER SAUCE

ZEST AND JUICE OF 1 LIME

1 TBSP HOT CHILLI SAUCE

1 TSP HONEY

½ TSP FIVE SPICE POWDER

2 TBSP VEGETABLE OIL

2 RED ONIONS, THINLY SLICED

2 GARLIC CLOVES, THINLY SLICED

1 RED PEPPER, THINLY SLICED

2 PAK CHOI, ROUGHLY CHOPPED

2 TSP SESAME SEEDS, TOASTED (OPTIONAL)

JASMINE RICE (SEE PAGE 13), TO SERVE

PORK AND PAK CHOI STIR-FRY

Ensure that you have all the vegetables and pork prepped before you start cooking. Once you get going, there's no time to be chopping again! Rather than cooking rice if it's too late, one of those packets of ready-cooked noodles is just fine at that hour. It's a one-pot meal and easy to put together in a rush. Pak choi is very convenient and bulks up a stir-fry when catering for a crowd.

SERVES 4

1 Place the pork and 1 tablespoon of the oyster sauce into a bowl and toss together.

2 Pour the remaining 2 tablespoons of the oyster sauce in a small bowl along with the lime juice, chilli sauce, honey and five spice powder. Mix together and set aside.

3 Heat 1 tablespoon of the vegetable oil in a large wok over a medium-high heat. Add the pork and quickly sear. Remove the pork from the wok and set aside.

4 Add the remaining 1 tablespoon of oil and then add the red onion, garlic and pepper and stir-fry for 2–3 minutes. Stir in the lime zest and the chilli and oyster sauce mix. Add the pak choi and return the pork back to the pan. Stir-fry for a further 1–2 minutes, until the pork is cooked through.

5 Sprinkle over some toasted sesame seeds (if using) and serve with jasmine rice.

FOR THE TOMATO SAUCE:
EXTRA VIRGIN OLIVE OIL
1 SMALL RED ONION, FINELY CHOPPED
1–1½ TSP HARISSA PASTE (DEPENDING ON HOW HOT YOU LIKE IT)
1 GARLIC CLOVE, CHOPPED
1 X 400G TIN CHOPPED TOMATOES
1 TSP HONEY
SALT AND FRESHLY GROUND BLACK PEPPER

FOR THE TOASTIES:
BUTTER
4 THICK SLICES WHITE ARTISAN BREAD
1 JAR OF ROASTED RED AND YELLOW PEPPERS, DRAINED
4–6 SLICES BRIE CHEESE
SALT AND FRESHLY GROUND BLACK PEPPER
BASIL LEAVES, TO GARNISH

1 To make the tomato sauce, heat a little olive oil in a saucepan over a medium-low heat. Add the onions and sauté for 6 minutes, until softened but not brown. Add the harissa paste and cook for about 1 minute, then stir in the garlic and cook for 1 minute more. Pour in the chopped tomatoes and honey. Simmer over a low heat for about 20 minutes, stirring from time to time. Check the seasoning.

2 To make the toasties, preheat the grill. Butter the bread on one side and toast under the grill on both sides until golden. Spoon the roasted peppers onto 2 of the pieces of toast and place a layer of Brie cheese on top. Season with salt and freshly ground black pepper. Place under the grill again until the cheese is melted, golden and bubbling. Remove from the grill, spoon some tomato sauce over the top and garnish with a few basil leaves. Place a slice of toast on top and slice in half. Serve immediately.

GRILLED ROAST PEPPER AND BRIE TOASTIES WITH OVER-THE-TOP TOMATO SAUCE

···············

Sometimes a stringy cheesy sandwich is just what's needed. It's also nice to have some spice, so I like to serve the toastie with a little tomato sauce that has a bit of a kick to it. Sealed in your fridge, the sauce will keep for up to 10 days and it freezes very well too, so store it in small portions and you have a sauce that you could also serve with spaghetti.

SERVES 2

SATURDAY AFTER-NOON

'MUSIC TO WATCH GIRLS BY' - ANDY WILLIAMS

'SUGAR, SUGAR' - THE ARCHIES

'BLUEBERRY HILL' - FATS DOMINO

CHAPTER

05 } FOOD FOR THE MATCH

I used to call this 'man food', but we all go to matches nowadays and there's nothing quite as welcoming as hearty, wholesome, hot food on a cold match day. Sport and food just seem to go together, but it has to be bold flavours and food that's sticky and messy! There are certain foods that are famous with certain sports, like strawberries with tennis or pies with football. It's all about 'grab' food, as a friend calls it.

In our household, sport can be a divider, especially when it comes to rugby or football. You can imagine the Italy vs. Ireland atmosphere in my house when the rugby is on!

1.5KG PORK SPARE RIBS
1 RED CHILLI, FINELY CHOPPED
2 TSP CORIANDER SEEDS, CRUSHED
1 LITRE POMEGRANATE JUICE

FOR THE SAUCE:
60G DARK BROWN SUGAR
1 X 2CM PIECE OF FRESH GINGER, GRATED
75ML POMEGRANATE MOLASSES
4 TBSP TOMATO KETCHUP
1 TSP GROUND CUMIN

FOR THE SALSA:
1 POMEGRANATE, DESEEDED
1 LARGE ORANGE, PEELED AND SEGMENTED
1 RED ONION, FINELY CHOPPED
SMALL BUNCH OF FRESH CORIANDER, ROUGHLY CHOPPED
JUICE OF 1 LIME

1 Preheat the oven to 170°C/fan 150°C/gas 3.

2 Place the ribs in a roasting tin. Sprinkle over the red chilli and coriander seeds and pour in the pomegranate juice. Cover with foil and roast for 1 hour 45 minutes, turning the ribs from time to time, until tender.

3 Place all the ingredients for the sauce into a small saucepan and bring to the boil. Reduce the heat and simmer for about 4 minutes, until a thick syrup forms.

4 When the ribs are done, pour off the pomegranate juice and brush the ribs with the sticky sauce. Cover and marinate for at least 1 hour, if not longer (12 hours is preferable). Allow the ribs to cool completely before placing them in the fridge.

5 To make the salsa, combine all the ingredients and set aside.

6 To finish the ribs, bring them to room temperature before cooking. Preheat the oven to 220°C/fan 200°C/gas 7.

7 Cook for 30 minutes, turning occasionally and basting from time to time with the sauce, until the ribs are sticky on the outside. Serve with the salsa.

PORK RIBS WITH ORANGE AND POMEGRANATE SALSA

· · · · · · · · · · · · · · ·

Sweet and sticky and oh so delicious – and even better when washed down with an ice cold beer.

SERVES 4

1 TSP FAST-ACTION YEAST

½ TSP SUGAR

120ML LUKEWARM WATER (MORE IF REQUIRED)

220G ITALIAN '00' OR STRONG WHITE FLOUR

1 TSP EXTRA VIRGIN OLIVE OIL, PLUS EXTRA FOR
  GREASING AND DRIZZLING

½ TSP SALT

700G NEW POTATOES, SKIN ON, COOKED AND SLICED
  VERY THINLY

2–3 GARLIC CLOVES, THINLY SLICED

6–7 SMALL SPRIGS OF FRESH ROSEMARY

2 TSP CHOPPED FRESH DILL

SALT AND FRESHLY GROUND BLACK PEPPER

1 To make the dough, mix the yeast and sugar in the lukewarm water and allow the yeast to activate. When the yeast foams, it's ready to use.

2 Sieve the flour into a mixing bowl and add the olive oil, salt and the yeast mixture. Mix to a loose dough, adding more flour or water as required. Knead until the dough is very pliable, which should take about 5 minutes using the dough hook of a stand mixer or 7–10 minutes by hand. Leave the dough to rise in a well-oiled bowl covered with cling film until the dough has trebled in size and is springy to the touch, which will take about 2 hours. This will rise best in a warm, draught-free place, e.g. a hot press or near a cooker or oven.

3 Preheat the oven to 220°C/fan 200°C/gas 7 or use a pizza stone on your barbecue. Lightly oil a baking sheet.

4 When the dough has risen, knock it back and place onto a lightly floured surface. Knead it again by hand for 2–3 minutes. Roll out or stretch the dough with your hands and place on the oiled baking sheet.

5 Drizzle the dough with extra virgin olive oil. Neatly arrange the slices of cooked potato on the dough and sprinkle the garlic over the top. Sprinkle some of the rosemary and dill over as well. Drizzle over a little more olive oil and season with salt and pepper. Cook for 20–25 minutes, until the pizza is cooked and the potatoes are golden and crisp. Sprinkle over the rest of the rosemary and dill and slide onto a wooden board to serve.

EASY PIZZA BOARDS

....

These must be thin pizza bases with thin layers of vegetable toppings, like sweet potatoes, leek, garlic and very thin slices of butternut squash with a good drizzle of olive oil. Lash on the herbs – I like to make a mix of 3 tablespoons chopped fresh parsley, 1 tablespoon chopped fresh dill and 1 teaspoon chopped fresh thyme with 1 teaspoon lemon zest.

MAKES ONE 30CM X 40CM RECTANGLE

EXTRA VIRGIN OLIVE OIL
1 LARGE LEEK, THINLY SLICED
2 X 225G PACKS OF READY-TO-ROLL PUFF PASTRY
200G CHORIZO SAUSAGE, DICED
100G MATURE CHEDDAR CHEESE, GRATED
1 EGG, LIGHTLY BEATEN
PAPRIKA, TO DUST

1 Preheat the oven to 220°C/fan 200°C/gas 7. Line a large baking tray with parchment paper.

2 To cook the leek, heat some extra virgin olive oil in a medium frying pan over a medium heat. Add the leek slices and sauté for about 5 minutes, until softened but not brown.

3 Lightly flour a work surface and roll out the pastry. Using a saucer as a template, cut out as many circles as possible (you should aim for 16 circles). Spoon about $1/2$ tablespoonful of the cooked leek in the centre of each pastry disc, then add some diced chorizo and Cheddar cheese. Brush a little of the beaten egg around the edge of the pastry and press the edges together to form a half moon. Repeat until all the circles are used.

4 Make a small incision on the top of each half moon. Place the pastries on the lined baking tray, brush the tops with beaten egg and sprinkle a fine dusting of paprika over the top.

5 Bake for 12–15 minutes, until well risen and golden. Transfer to a wire rack to cool slightly before serving.

CHORIZO AND CHEESE EMPANADILLAS

These are a very quick snack that friends can help with before you sit down to watch the game. Get them prepared ahead of time and all you have to do is put them into the oven to bake so that you can serve gorgeously hot empanadillas during the match without missing out on any of the excitement.

MAKES 16

100ML NATURAL YOGHURT

2 TSP HARISSA, PLUS EXTRA TO SERVE

3 SMALL CHICKEN FILLETS, SLICED INTO STRIPS

2 TBSP SUNFLOWER OIL

200G COOKED CHICKPEAS (TINNED IS FINE)

200ML HOT CHICKEN STOCK

1 TSP GROUND CUMIN

1 YELLOW PEPPER, ROASTED AND THINLY SLICED

4 TBSP CRÈME FRAÎCHE

SALT AND FRESHLY GROUND BLACK PEPPER

2 TBSP FINELY CHOPPED FRESH CORIANDER LEAVES,
   PLUS EXTRA SPRIGS TO GARNISH

LITTLE GEM OR BUTTER LETTUCE LEAVES, WASHED
   AND PAT DRY

3 RADISHES, SLICED

SPICY HARISSA CHICKEN IN LETTUCE CUPS (OR HUNGRY GUY'S PITAS)

Watching a match in our home isn't just a male-orientated event – we like to watch a little camogie as well! Serve these in lettuce leaves for those of us who are watching the calories, but pittas work too.

SERVES 4

1 Mix together the yoghurt and harissa in a large bowl. Add the chicken and toss to coat. Leave to marinate for at least 20 minutes.

2 Heat the oil in a large frying pan over a medium-high heat. Using tongs, remove the chicken fillets from the marinade, shaking off any excess, and add to the pan. Sauté for 2–3 minutes on each side, until golden. Transfer to a plate and set aside.

3 Add the chickpeas and hot stock to the frying pan as well as the ground cumin and simmer for 4–5 minutes, until the chickpeas are heated through. Stir in the roasted yellow pepper and crème fraîche. Return the chicken to the pan and simmer for a further 3 minutes, then check the seasoning and add the chopped coriander. Allow to cool until just warm, then spoon into the lettuce leaves and place on a serving platter. Top with the radish slices and coriander sprigs and serve immediately.

FOR THE SALAD:

8 CHERRY TOMATOES, HALVED

½ CUCUMBER, PEELED AND SLICED INTO RIBBONS

JUICE OF 1 LEMON (RETAIN A LITTLE TO DRIZZLE OVER THE AVOCADO)

4 TBSP EXTRA VIRGIN OLIVE OIL

FOR THE PITAS:

1 TBSP EXTRA VIRGIN OLIVE OIL, PLUS EXTRA FOR FRYING

1 TSP GROUND CUMIN

1 TSP CHOPPED FRESH ROSEMARY

300G BEEF SIRLOIN

SALT AND FRESHLY GROUND BLACK PEPPER

1 RIPE AVOCADO, PEELED, STONE REMOVED AND SLICED, AND DRIZZLED WITH A LITTLE LEMON JUICE

4 PITA BREADS, WARMED AND SLICED OPEN

50G ROCKET OR YOUR FAVOURITE SALAD LEAVES

SOUR CREAM, TO SERVE

1 To prepare the salad, place the tomatoes and cucumber ribbons in a bowl. Whisk the lemon juice and olive oil together and pour a little over the salad.

2 To prepare the pitas, mix the oil, cumin and rosemary together and brush over the beef. Allow to marinate for 10 minutes.

3 Heat a large heavy-based frying pan with some extra virgin olive oil over a high heat. Using a pair of tongs, place the beef into the pan and sear on all sides, then cook for 3–4 minutes, depending on how you like your steak (2–3 minutes for medium rare or 4–5 minutes for well done). Sprinkle with a little salt and freshly ground black pepper. Remove the beef from the pan, cover and rest for 5 minutes, then slice into strips about 2cm wide.

4 Spoon some of the avocado into the pitas, then slide the steak in and pack with the cucumber salad, rocket leaves and the remaining avocado. Serve with sour cream.

'BEEF IT UP' PITAS

....

These pitas will certainly fill the gap in the hunger department. Thinly sliced pork fillet is also very tasty in the pitas, served with a mustard dressing and sautéed leeks.

SERVES 4

CHAPTER

06

AFTERNOON TEA

....

I love afternoon tea because you can be creative with gorgeous colours, flowers, floral cake stands, beautiful teapots and a mishmash of teacups on fabulous linen tablecloths or even vintage trays.

It's a sweet and savoury meal, with tables laden with shortbread biscuits, pretty cupcakes with crystallised violets on top, stands with divine Victoria sponge cakes and layers of fresh berries, rose petals and cream, or strawberry mousse in shot glasses using your granny's favourite little teaspoons.

Here's how to make a great cup of tea, as taught to me by my grandmother, Kitty, many years ago. First, empty the kettle and pour in fresh cold water. Make sure that the water boils. Rinse the teapots and cups or mugs with the boiling water. Add the loose tea to the pot, pour over the boiling water and allow the tea to infuse for 4 minutes. Use a tea strainer for sieving out the leaves.

TO ENERGISE	Rosehip, lemon verbena, pepper-mint or borage or a combination of some of these
TO KEEP CALM	Camomile, lavender, basil and orange
TO EASE A HEADACHE	Rosemary and peppermint
TO SOOTHE A SORE THROAT	Sage, cayenne, peppermint or rosehip or a combination of some of these

TISANES

When I visited a farm near New York a few years ago, I was so inspired by the wonderful tisanes that I was offered. I try to have one every day – there's a herbal tea for almost any occasion. Here are a few of my suggestions for serving a refreshing afternoon tea. Generally, 1 teaspoon of dried herbs is equal to 1 table-spoon of fresh herbs, but it's really down to your preference.

ORANGE, ROSEMARY AND GINGER

Place 3 or 4 orange slices, 2 small sprigs of fresh rosemary and 2 thin slices of fresh ginger into a teapot. Pour over about 600ml boiling water and infuse for 7 minutes. Stir in a little honey if you like.

CAMOMILE, LAVENDER AND MINT

Place 3 or 4 mint leaves, 1 tablespoon of dried camomile flowers and leaves and $1/4$ – $1/2$ teaspoon of dried culinary lavender into a teapot. Pour over about 600ml boiling water and infuse for 5 minutes. (Just one note: ensure that you purchase culinary lavender.)

RASPBERRY, FENNEL AND HONEY

Place 7 or 8 fresh raspberries and $1/2$ teaspoon of fennel seeds into a teapot. Pour over 600ml boiling water and infuse for 7–10 minutes, then stir in a little honey. This is one of my favourites, as it restores energy and is also very calming.

FOR THE CAKES:
180G BUTTER, SOFTENED, PLUS EXTRA MELTED BUTTER
  FOR GREASING
180G CASTER SUGAR
ZEST OF 1 LIME
3 EGGS
180G SELF-RAISING FLOUR, PLUS EXTRA FOR DUSTING

FOR THE LIME BUTTERCREAM:
350G ICING SUGAR, SIEVED
180G BUTTER, SOFTENED
ZEST AND JUICE OF 1 LIME

1 LIME, THINLY SLICED, TO DECORATE

1 Preheat the oven to 180°C/fan 160°C/gas 4. Brush a 12-hole mini sandwich tin or muffin tray with melted butter and dust with flour.

2 To make the cakes, cream the butter, sugar and lime zest in a mixer until pale and fluffy. Add the eggs one at a time, mixing well after each addition. Fold in the flour. Carefully spoon the batter into the muffin tray until each well is two-thirds full. Bake for about 15 minutes – when a skewer inserted into the centre of the cakes comes out clean, the cakes are done. Cool the cakes slightly in the tray before transferring to a wire rack to cool completely.

3 To make the lime buttercream, cream together the icing sugar, butter, lime zest and 2 tablespoons of the lime juice in a mixer until pale and fluffy.

4 Spread the lime buttercream on top of 6 of the cakes and place the remaining 6 cakes on top. Pipe or spread a little more buttercream on top of the finished cakes and decorate with lime slices.

MINI LIME LAYER CAKES

These mini cakes are a nice little surprise to add to the cake stand. They are our Mad Hatter tea party cakes – fun and funky – but you'll love the lime and the sweetness. If you feel that they are too tall, slice them a little before spreading on the buttercream.

MAKES 6

CHOCOLATE AND ORANGE TARTLETS

· · · · · · · · · · · · · · ·

Sometimes, even at weekends, time is too short to make your own pastry, so good-quality ready-made pastry is perfectly fine. If you have time to make your own, use the sesame pastry on page 142. The small tartlets are the perfect bite-sized treat.

**MAKES 24 SMALL OR
8 X 10CM TARTLETS**

MELTED BUTTER, FOR GREASING
PLAIN FLOUR, FOR DUSTING
375G READY-TO-ROLL SHORTCRUST PASTRY
250G DARK CHOCOLATE
250ML DOUBLE CREAM
2 TBSP ORANGE LIQUEUR
ORANGE ZEST STRIPS, TO DECORATE

1 Preheat the oven to 190°C/fan 170°C/gas 5. Brush 2 x 12-hole mini tartlet trays (or any other size that you may be using) with melted butter and dust with flour.

2 Dust a work surface with flour and roll out the pastry into a 20cm circle. Using a scone cutter to match the size of the tins that you're using, stamp out pastry discs and line the trays with them. Line the pastry cases with parchment paper, fill with baking beans and bake blind for about 8 minutes, depending on the size. Remove the paper and baking beans and return to the oven for a further 2 minutes. Allow to cool completely.

3 Meanwhile, melt the chocolate in a bowl set over a saucepan of simmering water (ban marie), taking care not to let the water touch the bottom of the bowl. Combine the melted chocolate with the double cream and orange liqueur. Pour into a jug, then carefully pour into the tartlet cases. Allow to set at room temperature and decorate with the orange strips.

220G BUTTER, SOFTENED

150G GOLDEN CASTER SUGAR

1 TSP VANILLA EXTRACT

½ TSP CARDAMOM SEEDS, GROUND IN A PESTLE
  AND MORTAR

260G PLAIN FLOUR

1 EGG WHITE

100G CHOCOLATE, MELTED

1 Preheat the oven to 180°C/fan 160°C/gas 4. Line 2 baking trays with parchment paper.

2 Place the butter, sugar, vanilla and crushed cardamom seeds into a mixing bowl and cream together until pale and fluffy. Fold in the flour.

3 In a separate clean, dry bowl, beat the egg white until it's just foamy. Fold into the biscuit dough.

4 Using damp hands, divide the dough into 24 long, thin, cylindrical shapes and place onto the trays, allowing plenty of room for them to spread during baking.

5 Bake for 10-12 minutes, until they're lightly golden around the edges. Leave on the tray for 5 minutes to set, then transfer to a wire rack to cool completely.

6 Line 2 more baking trays with parchment paper. Dip the biscuits, one at a time, into the melted chocolate to coat one end, allowing any excess to drip away. Lay them on the lined trays. Chill in the fridge very briefly to set the chocolate. Alternatively, you can set out a pretty bowl of melted warm chocolate for everyone to dip the biscuits into.

CARDAMOM VIENNESE BISCUITS WITH CHOCOLATE DIPPING SAUCE

Cardamom blends very well with chocolate. You'll just want to keep on dipping these into the chocolate – it's a bit like having chocolate fondue for afternoon tea.

MAKES 24

AFTERNOON TEA SANDWICHES THREE WAYS

....

Long gone are the days of soggy cucumber sandwiches. Petite sandwiches with interesting fillings are a popular classic to have on your afternoon tea menu. Choose bread that will contrast with the filling that you're using. The rye soda bread on page 155 is an easy base for sandwiches. Link sandwiches together with sturdy rosemary stalks or interesting skewers. To keep the sandwiches from drying out, sprinkle a little cold water over them, cover with parchment paper and then cover again with plastic wrap and keep in the fridge until needed.

CHARGRILLED COURGETTE, ROASTED PEPPER AND WATERCRESS

....

MAKES 4

8 THIN SLICES OF WHITE BREAD

2 TBSP BASIL PESTO

1 COURGETTE, THINLY SLICED LENGTHWAYS AND CHARGRILLED

2 RED PEPPERS, DESEEDED, HALVED AND ROASTED

BUNCH OF WATERCRESS

Place the white bread on a cutting board and spread over the pesto. Arrange the courgette slices on 4 slices of the bread. Thinly slice the red peppers and place on top of the courgettes. Top with the watercress and the remaining bread. Slice the sandwiches into triangles or 3 thin fingers.

TROUT WITH CUCUMBER RIBBONS AND CITRUS MAYONNAISE

....

MAKES 6 OPEN-FACED SANDWICHES

4 TBSP MAYONNAISE

ZEST OF ½ ORANGE

ZEST AND JUICE OF ½ LEMON

6 SLICES OF RYE BREAD

1 CUCUMBER, PEELED INTO RIBBONS

1 TBSP OLIVE OIL

125G SMOKED TROUT FILLET, SLICED

FRESHLY GROUND BLACK PEPPER

FRESH DILL SPRIGS, TO GARNISH

Mix together the mayonnaise, orange zest and lemon zest and juice. Spread the citrus mayonnaise on the bread, then pile on the cucumber ribbons, drizzle with a little olive oil and arrange a twist of trout on top. Season with freshly ground black pepper. Arrange a sprig of dill on top of each open sandwich and place on a platter, ready to be served.

BLUEBERRIES, LIME CREAM CHEESE AND HONEY

....

MAKES 9

4–5 THIN SLICES OF SODA BREAD

4 TBSP CREAM CHEESE

ZEST OF ½ LIME, PLUS EXTRA TO DECORATE

1 TBSP HONEY

50G BLUEBERRIES, WASHED

Using a 3cm daisy cutter, stamp out shapes from the bread. Mix the cream cheese, lime zest and honey in a small bowl and spread over the bread. Arrange the blueberries on top. Sprinkle over a little lime zest. Arrange on a platter and serve immediately.

BLACKBERRY AND PEAR CAKE WITH HAZELNUT AND HONEY TOPPING

....

I can't remember how many times I have said certain recipes are my favourite, but this is my favourite of all favourites. It's a great one to serve when you have a few friends over and need a more substantial cake. Serve it with a spoon of cream or even as dessert for a casual evening when your good friends are over for supper.

SERVES 8–10

FOR THE CAKE:
180G CASTER SUGAR
160G BUTTER, SOFTENED
4 LARGE EGGS
250G PLAIN FLOUR
2 TSP BAKING POWDER
120G NATURAL YOGHURT
ZEST OF ½ ORANGE
2 RIPE PEARS, PEELED AND THINLY SLICED
100G BLACKBERRIES, WASHED
2 TBSP HONEY

FOR THE HAZELNUT TOPPING:
70G BUTTER
100G FLOUR
70G LIGHT BROWN SUGAR
60G HAZELNUTS, ROUGHLY CHOPPED
ZEST OF ½ ORANGE
1 TSP GROUND CINNAMON

MASCARPONE OR CREAM, TO SERVE

1 Preheat the oven to 180°C/fan 160°C/gas 4. Butter and line a 24cm springform tin with baking parchment.

2 To make the topping, melt the butter in a pot and mix in the flour, brown sugar, hazelnuts, orange zest and cinnamon.

3 To make the cake, cream together the sugar and butter until fluffy. Add the eggs one at a time, mixing well after each addition. Fold in the flour and baking powder and stir in the yoghurt.

4 Spoon two-thirds of the cake batter into the tin and use a spatula to spread it evenly.

5 Arrange one-third of the pear slices and one-third of the blackberries over the batter and sprinkle with one-third of the hazelnut topping. Spoon over the rest of the cake batter and spread it evenly with a spatula. Arrange the rest of the pears and blackberries on top and sprinkle over the rest of the hazelnut topping.

6 Bake for about 40 minutes, or until a skewer inserted into the centre comes out clean. While still warm, drizzle over the honey. Allow the cake to cool before releasing it from the tin. Serve with mascarpone or cream.

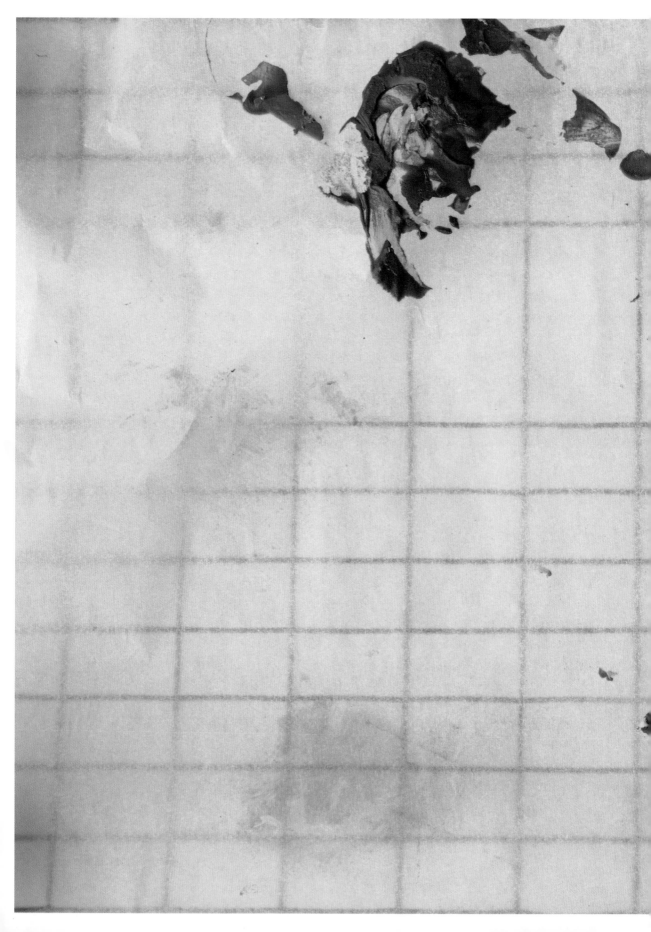

07 } BAKING DAY

I love baking, especially on rainy days. There is nothing more comforting than having some music or a good radio programme cranked up in the background when the mixer is humming happily on the kitchen counter. In our kitchen, we have a baking drawer filled with special Christmas biscuit cutters, baking ingredients like vanilla paste, cocoa, pretty sprinkles or cake tin linings and those gorgeous little cupcake cases that I just can't resist buying when I'm out and about.

FOR THE CAKE:
MELTED BUTTER, FOR GREASING
180G CASTER SUGAR
4 EGGS
200G SELF-RAISING FLOUR
1 TSP BAKING POWDER
½ TSP GROUND CINNAMON
½ TSP GROUND NUTMEG
½ ALLSPICE
250G PINEAPPLE PIECES IN SYRUP, FINELY DICED
150G COOKED BEETROOT, PEELED AND GRATED
100G WALNUTS, ROUGHLY CHOPPED
200ML SUNFLOWER OIL
12 WALNUT HALVES, TO DECORATE

FOR THE ICING:
100G BUTTER, SOFTENED
1 TSP VANILLA ESSENCE
220G ICING SUGAR, SIEVED

BEETROOT AND PINEAPPLE CAKE

....

You might think this sounds unusual, but it's very moist and the grated beetroot gives it an earthy flavour. Use disposable gloves when grating the beetroot, otherwise your hands will be a lovely shade of pink all week.

MAKES 1 X 24CM CAKE

1 Preheat the oven to 170°C/fan 150°C/gas 3. Brush a 24cm springform tin with melted butter and line the base with parchment paper.

2 Whisk the caster sugar and eggs together until thick and creamy. Sieve the flour, baking powder, cinnamon, nutmeg and allspice into a large bowl, then carefully fold into the sugar and eggs. Stir in the pineapple, beetroot, chopped walnuts and oil and mix well.

3 Pour the batter into the springform tin and bake for 45-50 minutes, until a skewer inserted into the centre comes out clean. Remove from the oven and cool in the tin for a while before removing to a cooling rack.

4 To make the icing, beat the butter and vanilla until smooth. Add the icing sugar in spoonfuls and beat until smooth. Spread the icing over the top of the cooled cake, pipe a swirl of icing around the edge and arrange the walnut halves on top.

FOR THE CAKE:

150G LIGHT BROWN SUGAR

150ML SUNFLOWER OIL

3 EGGS

1 RIPE MEDIUM BANANA, MASHED

175G SELF-RAISING FLOUR, SIEVED

1 TSP BAKING POWDER

1 TSP MIXED SPICE

100G GRATED PARSNIP

75G HAZELNUTS, ROUGHLY CHOPPED

FOR THE ICING:

100G ICING SUGAR, SIEVED

70G BUTTER, SOFTENED

75G CREAM CHEESE

1 TBSP MAPLE SYRUP

12 WHOLE HAZELNUTS, TOASTED AND ROUGHLY CHOPPED

PARSNIP AND HAZELNUT TEA LOAF

....

Irish carrots are especially sweet, so you could use them instead of parsnips. The banana in the recipe ensures that the loaf doesn't dry out – it will keep for almost a week if you can resist it for that long!

MAKES 1 LARGE LOAF

1 Preheat the oven to 170°C/fan 150°C/gas 3. Line a 2lb loaf tin with parchment paper.

2 Using an electric beater, mix the brown sugar, oil and eggs together until light in colour, then add the mashed banana. Fold in the flour, baking powder and mixed spice, followed by the grated parsnip and chopped hazelnuts. Pour into the prepared tin and bake for 45–50 minutes, until a skewer inserted into the centre comes out clean. Cool completely before removing from the loaf tin.

3 To make the icing, beat together the icing sugar and butter with an electric mixer until pale and fluffy. Gradually beat in the cream cheese a spoonful at a time. When the cake is cooled, spread on the icing. Drizzle over the maple syrup and sprinkle with the chopped hazelnuts.

1 TSP FAST-ACTION DRIED YEAST

3 TBSP CASTER SUGAR

100ML WARM WATER

220G STRONG WHITE FLOUR, PLUS EXTRA FOR DUSTING

2 TSP GROUND CINNAMON

¼ TSP SALT

2 EGGS

50G SOFTENED UNSALTED BUTTER, PLUS EXTRA MELTED BUTTER FOR BRUSHING

8 WALNUTS, FINELY CHOPPED

ICING SUGAR, FOR DUSTING

1 Brush a deep, fluted, loose-bottomed 20cm flan tin with melted butter.

2 Place the yeast in a large mixing bowl. Add 1 tablespoon of the sugar and pour in the water, then stir until the yeast and sugar have dissolved. Add 120g of the flour and mix well with a wooden spoon to form a soft dough. Cover and leave in a warm place for about 1 hour, or until the dough has doubled in size.

3 While the dough is rising, mix the remaining 100g flour with 1 teaspoon of the cinnamon and the salt in a small bowl.

4 When the dough has risen, add the flour, cinnamon and salt mixture and 1 lightly beaten egg into the dough, mixing until it comes together. Add in the butter with a wooden spoon until well combined. Cover the bowl and leave to rise again for 1 hour. When the dough has doubled in size, knock it back to release the air.

5 Lightly dust a surface with flour and place the dough on top. Push the dough out with your fingertips to flatten it and stretch it into a rectangle 25cm x 30cm and about 3mm thick.

6 Lightly beat the remaining egg in a small bowl and brush the dough all over with the egg wash. Mix together 2 tablespoons caster sugar, 1 teaspoon cinnamon and the chopped walnuts in a small bowl, then sprinkle this over the dough. Roll up the dough starting from one of the longer sides, then cut the roll into slices about 3cm thick (you should get 12-14 slices). Arrange them, cut side up, inside the prepared flan tin with one in the centre. Cover and leave to rise in a warm place for 45 minutes to 1 hour, until the rolls are almost doubled in size.

6 Preheat the oven to 200°C/fan 180°C/gas 6.

7 Bake the rolls for 18-20 minutes, until golden brown. Allow to cool slightly, then transfer to a cooling rack. Brush melted butter over the warm rolls, then dust with a little more cinnamon and icing sugar.

CINNAMON AND WALNUT ROLLS

The whole family will love these rolls and they are so easy to take on picnics or a hike in the country. Fresh is best in this case – there is nothing nicer than freshly baked yeast rolls or bread when invited to brunch. The whole house seems to be filled with the memorable aroma.

MAKES 12-14

2 TBSP GOLDEN CASTER SUGAR

2 TSP FAST-ACTION DRIED YEAST

125ML WARM MILK

3 EGGS

450G STRONG WHITE FLOUR

½ TSP SALT

3–4 CARDAMOM PODS

160G BUTTER, SOFTENED

100G CHOCOLATE DROPS

SUNFLOWER OIL, FOR GREASING

1 EGG, LIGHTLY BEATEN

1 Dissolve the sugar, yeast and warm milk in the bowl of a stand mixer and allow the yeast to foam. Insert the whisk attachment and add 3 eggs, one at a time, mixing well after each addition. Change to the dough hook attachment and add half of the flour and the salt. Mix the dough on a low speed for 5 minutes. Add the remaining flour and mix again for a further 5 minutes. Place the dough in a large bowl, cover loosely with plastic wrap and place in the fridge for at least 8 hours, or overnight (you can keep it in the fridge for up to 24 hours).

2 Meanwhile, toast the cardamom pods in a dry frying pan until they burst open. Discard the husks and crush the seeds in a pestle and mortar.

3 Allow the dough to come to room temperature. Beat the butter into the dough, adding 1–2 tablespoons of flour if you feel that it's too sticky. Add the crushed cardamom seeds and chocolate drops to the dough. Place in a bowl, cover loosely with oiled plastic wrap and allow to rise for 2 hours, until it doubles in size.

4 Brush a brioche tray or moulds with oil. Knock back the dough and knead it briefly, then divide the dough into 10–12 large balls and place in the oiled tins.

5 Loosely cover with oiled plastic wrap and leave in a warm place for 25–30 minutes, until well risen.

6 Preheat the oven to 190°C/fan 170°C/gas 5.

7 Brush with the lightly beaten egg and bake for 25 minutes, until golden brown and cooked through. Allow to cool slightly in the tins before transferring to a wire rack.

CHOCOLATE AND CARDAMOM BRIOCHE BUNS

••••••••••••••••••••••••••••

The children will be so pleased with themselves after mastering these buns. Serve them for Sunday brunch or prepare mini ones for a casual coffee morning. If you don't have special brioche moulds, use a loaf tin.

MAKES 10–12

ORANGE AND ALMOND POLENTA SQUARES, p.89

MELTED BUTTER, FOR GREASING
4 EGGS
300G GOLDEN CASTER SUGAR
170ML RAPESEED OIL
100ML MILK
280G SELF-RAISING FLOUR
100G PORRIDGE OATS
½ TSP GROUND GINGER
½ TSP SALT
2 MEDIUM CARROTS, GRATED
1 PEAR, PEELED AND FINELY DICED
100G DRIED MANGO, FINELY DICED
ICING SUGAR, FOR DUSTING

MANGO AND CARROT CAKE

....

This will impress when the girls are coming around for an afternoon chat. That said, my children love to bake this cake as muffins. They add blueberries (about 3 tablespoons) for extra juiciness and goodness.

MAKES 1 X 23CM CAKE

1 Preheat the oven to 170°C/fan 150°C/gas 3. Brush a 23cm springform cake tin with melted butter and line the base with parchment paper.

2 Whisk the eggs, sugar, oil and milk together until thick and pale. Fold in the flour, porridge oats, ginger and salt, then stir in the grated carrot, diced pear and mango. Spoon the batter into the cake tin and bake for about 30 minutes, until lightly golden and a skewer inserted into the centre comes out clean.

3 Cool on a wire rack, then remove from the tin and dust with icing sugar.

FOR THE CAKE:
**200G BUTTER, SOFTENED, PLUS EXTRA MELTED
  BUTTER FOR GREASING**
180G CASTER SUGAR
4 EGGS
180G PLAIN FLOUR, PLUS EXTRA FOR DUSTING
100G POLENTA
4 TBSP GROUND ALMONDS
2 TSP BAKING POWDER
ZEST AND JUICE OF 1 ORANGE

FOR THE ORANGE TOPPING:
ZEST AND JUICE OF 2 ORANGES
120G CASTER SUGAR

1 Preheat the oven to 180°C/fan 160°C/gas 4. Line the base of a rectangular 20cm x 30cm baking tin with parchment paper, brush the sides with melted butter and dust with flour.

2 Cream the butter and sugar together until light and fluffy. Add the eggs one as a time, mixing well after each addition.

3 Combine the flour, polenta, ground almonds and baking powder, then fold into the butter and sugar mixture. Add the orange juice and zest and mix until just combined.

4 Pour the batter into the prepared tin and spread it evenly. Bake for about 40 minutes, checking from time to time. When a skewer inserted into the centre comes out clean, the cake is done.

5 To make the topping, stir the orange zest, juice and sugar together in a small jug. While the cake is still hot, pour over the orange and sugar topping. Allow the cake to cool, then slice into squares.

ORANGE AND ALMOND POLENTA SQUARES

....

Not only is this an easy tray bake to make for school fairs and cake sales, but it's delicious served slightly warm with a little amaretto cream and syrupy cardamom orange segments. These are really filling too because of the combination of polenta and almonds.

MAKES 16 SQUARES

SATURDAY NIGHT

'EVERYBODY EATS WHEN THEY COME TO MY HOUSE' - CAB CALLOWAY

'MAMBO ITALIANO' - ROSEMARY CLOONEY

'BAUBLES, BANGLES AND BEADS' - ELIANE ELIAS

CHAPTER 08 { TAPAS NIGHT

Eating little bits of interesting foods really appeals to me. It's like testing new recipes, when we only taste a little at a time. At least that's what I try to convince myself – then I end up going for extra-long walks to get back into some kind of shape!

I love the casual, carefree style of a tapas evening because there's such a great variety of sunshine flavours. The best part is that all age groups love tapas, so having tapas at an 18th birthday party is as cool as having your close friends over for an evening of enjoying different tasty treats. There's also a good balance of hot and cold, so advance prep can be done, which is helpful when inviting friends over.

A few shot glasses of roasted garlic, bean and cheese dips with tall breadsticks for dipping lined up on a board, baked new potatoes stuffed with artichokes, bowls of olives with orange zest and dill, prawns with spicy tomato sauce and jugs of sangria will get your evening off to a great start – you might even think you're in Spain. *Olé!*

Just remember that the recipes in this chapter are tapas portions (small), so you'll have to choose a selection of tapas for an evening. Try five or six different ones to keep everyone in good form and the party going.

MUSSELS WITH SAFFRON AND CREAM

....

I don't think we use mussels enough when entertaining – they are so quick to prepare. Ensure that they are clean and rinsed a good few times and throw out any mussels that have opened before they are cooked and ones that are still closed after they are cooked. A little saffron adds a special something to any dish. Expensive as it is, it's worth it to have some in your store cupboard.

SERVES 4

400G MUSSELS
1 TBSP EXTRA VIRGIN OLIVE OIL
1 SMALL ONION, FINELY CHOPPED
1 GARLIC CLOVE, SLICED
PINCH OF SAFFRON STRANDS, SOAKED IN 1 TBSP WATER
4 TBSP DRY WHITE WINE
1 BAY LEAF
50ML DOUBLE CREAM
2 TBSP CHOPPED FRESH PARSLEY, TO GARNISH
1 LEMON, THINLY SLICED, TO SERVE

1 Clean the mussels under cold running water and remove any beards. Discard any mussels that are open and that don't close when lightly tapped on the counter. Rinse twice again.

2 Heat the extra virgin olive oil in a large saucepan over a medium heat. Add the onion and sauté for about 5 minutes. Add the garlic and saffron and cook for 1 minute more. Pour in the wine, add the bay leaf and bring to boil with the lid on. Add the mussels to the steaming pot, cover with a lid and leave to steam for 2–3 minutes. Once cooked, the mussels will open. Ensure that you discard any mussels that remain closed.

3 Pour in the cream, cook for 1 minute and stir well. Spoon the mussels into small serving bowls, ladling over some of the cooking juices as well as some garlic and onion. Sprinkle over the chopped parsley and serve immediately with lemon slices.

GARLIC ARTICHOKES AND MUSHROOMS, p.95

ALMENDRAS FRITAS, p.96

ROASTED GRAPES WITH JAMÓN SERRANO, p.96

GARLIC ARTICHOKES AND MUSHROOMS

....

3 TBSP EXTRA VIRGIN OLIVE OIL

200G CHESTNUT MUSHROOMS, WIPED CLEAN, STEMS
  REMOVED AND SLICED INTO QUARTERS

4 GARLIC CLOVES, SLICED

1 TSP SMOKED PAPRIKA

285G MARINATED ARTICHOKES, CUT INTO WEDGES

ZEST AND JUICE OF 1 LEMON

SALT AND FRESHLY GROUND BLACK PEPPER

1 TBSP CHOPPED CHIVES, TO GARNISH

Everyone loves the sweet aroma of garlic cooking. In this recipe, it melts together with the mushrooms and artichokes. The lemon forms a great dressing with the extra virgin olive oil. Try serving these delicious mushrooms in a selection of lettuce leaves and top with small crunchy herb croutons for lunch, and present them on a large shallow bowl so everyone can tuck in.

1 Heat the extra virgin olive oil in a shallow frying pan over a medium heat. Add the mushrooms and cook gently for about 2 minutes. Add the garlic and smoked paprika and sauté for 1 minute more, stirring occasionally. Add the artichoke wedges and the lemon zest and juice and remove from the heat. Taste for seasoning.

2 Allow the flavours to infuse for about 2 hours at room temperature. Sprinkle over the chopped chives and serve with small forks.

SERVES 4

ROASTED GRAPES WITH JAMÓN SERRANO

. . . .

The roasted grapes are simple and can be added to salads or served on a cheese board. They keep in the fridge for a couple of days as well. Thin wedges of figs or peaches are also delicious when lightly roasted this way.

SERVES 6-8

500G RED SEEDLESS GRAPES, DIVIDED INTO SMALL BUNCHES
2 TBSP SHERRY VINEGAR
8–10 THIN SLICES OF JAMÓN SERRANO

1 Preheat the oven to 200°C/fan 180°C/gas 6. Line a baking sheet with parchment paper.

2 Put bunches of red grapes on the tray and drizzle with the sherry vinegar. Roast for about 10 minutes on one side and then turn them over and roast for about 8 minutes on the other side. (The cooking time depends on the size and sweetness of the grapes – sweeter grapes can burst open if they're left in the oven for too long, as they're laden with lovely juice.) Baste the grapes from time to time. They will begin to soften and caramelise.

3 Arrange the slices of jamón serrano on a platter alongside the grapes and serve.

ALMENDRAS FRITAS

. . . .

Fried almonds are one of the favourites in my tapas class. We can't stop everyone (including myself) from eating them before the end of the class! We now prepare them as the very last dish, as that ensures everyone can have some – you may also need to do this. Try different types of nuts. Hazelnuts are a good choice, as are macadamias. You may need to double the recipe, as these are so moreish!

SERVES 4-6

25G BUTTER
4 TBSP EXTRA VIRGIN OLIVE OIL
200G WHOLE, BLANCHED ALMONDS
2 TBSP ROCK OR SEA SALT
¼ TSP CAYENNE

1 Line a plate with kitchen paper.

2 Heat the butter and extra virgin olive oil in a frying pan over a medium heat and sauté the almonds, stirring, until they're light golden brown. Transfer the almonds to the lined plate to drain slightly, then place in a bowl, sprinkle with the salt and cayenne and toss to combine.

3 Serve warm or at room temperature. These will keep in an airtight container for up to 1 week – though they never last that long in my home!

4 TBSP EXTRA VIRGIN OLIVE OIL
4 LARGE POTATOES, PEELED AND CUT INTO 2CM CHUNKS
SALT

FOR THE SAUCE:
EXTRA VIRGIN OLIVE OIL
1 ONION, FINELY CHOPPED
1 X 400G TIN CHOPPED PLUM TOMATOES
5 DROPS TABASCO SAUCE, OR TO TASTE
1 TBSP WHOLEGRAIN MUSTARD
SALT AND SUGAR, TO SEASON

PATATAS BRAVAS

....

You can't have a tapas evening without a favourite classic. This is my take on it, as there are so many different versions. The tomato sauce can be served over roasted parsnips or turnips or with steamed celery and broccoli.

SERVES 6-8

1 To make the sauce, heat a medium saucepan with some extra virgin olive oil. Add the onion and sauté for 5-6 minutes over a medium heat, until soft but not brown. Add the chopped plum tomatoes, Tabasco and mustard and bring to the boil. Reduce the heat and simmer for about 15 minutes, or until the sauce has thickened. Check for seasoning, adding salt or sugar.

2 Meanwhile, heat 4 tablespoons of extra virgin olive oil in a large frying pan over a medium heat. Add the potato chunks and shallow fry for 6-7 minutes, until golden brown and cooked. Drain the potatoes on kitchen paper, then place in a shallow serving bowl and sprinkle with salt. Spoon over the heated sauce and serve immediately.

225G MINCED PORK
225G LEAN MINCED BEEF
1 ONION, FINELY CHOPPED
2 GARLIC CLOVES, FINELY CHOPPED
4 TBSP BREADCRUMBS
1 TSP CHOPPED FRESH THYME
½ TSP SMOKED PAPRIKA
SALT AND FRESHLY GROUND BLACK PEPPER
1 EGG, BEATEN
EXTRA VIRGIN OLIVE OIL
SAFFRON RICE, TO SERVE

FOR THE SAUCE:
EXTRA VIRGIN OLIVE OIL
1 ONION, FINELY CHOPPED
1 GARLIC CLOVE, FINELY CHOPPED
1 RED CHILLI, FINELY CHOPPED
1 X 400G TIN CHOPPED TOMATOES
250ML VEGETABLE STOCK
2 TBSP TOMATO PURÉE
½ TSP CASTER SUGAR
SALT AND FRESHLY GROUND BLACK PEPPER

1 To make the meatballs, first line a plate with parchment paper. Place the pork, beef, onion and garlic into a large bowl and mix well. Mix in the breadcrumbs, thyme, paprika and some salt and pepper, then add the beaten egg and mix thoroughly. Using wet hands, shape into balls the size of golf balls. Place on the lined plate.

2 Heat some oil in a large frying pan over a medium heat. Shallow fry the meatballs in batches, turning from time to time, until golden brown all over. Keep warm and set aside.

3 Meanwhile, to make the sauce, heat a large saucepan with some extra virgin olive oil over a medium heat. Add the onion and sauté for 7–8 minutes, until softened but not browned. Add the garlic and chilli and cook for 1 minute more.

4 Add the tomatoes, stock, tomato purée, sugar and some salt and pepper. Reduce the heat to low and simmer for 10–12 minutes, stirring from time to time. Increase the heat slightly, add the meatballs to the sauce and simmer for 8–10 minutes, until the meatballs are heated through and fully cooked. Serve with saffron rice.

ALBONDIGAS

....

These mini meatballs are so popular with my family. Team them with saffron rice or stir a mix of chopped fennel and lemon zest through the rice. You can also add a few sliced olives to the tomato sauce as well as a dash of sherry.
SERVES 4

CHAPTER
09 | DINNER PARTY

As a host, the hardest thing about a dinner party is where to start! My advice is to choose recipes that you have made before and don't take too much on. It's usually a good idea to have a maximum of two last-minute dishes to prepare, whether it's making a risotto or steaming broccoli.

In my cookery school, I always advise to plan for colour and texture too. Everything white, such as risotto, fish pie and panna cotta, is pale and soft, so I add in crispy textures with salads, fruits and roasts, and I add colour in many forms – green, orange, red and yellow fruits and veg are all vibrant on plates.

To start, create some ambience. Dim the lights, hang up fairy lights in the gazebo or place groups of candles in lanterns in focal places (the low lighting saves having to do too much dusting beforehand too). Create a music play list and have some nibbles and drinks ready before your guests arrive.

Send the invites out three weeks beforehand – it doesn't matter if you send them via email or snail mail, just make them a little different. Decide what recipes you want to make, then make a list and shop on the Thursday before your Saturday evening party. And it might sound obvious, but check that you have enough cutlery and delph, especially glasses.

Set up a cocktail bar for everyone to help themselves. You could even place three or four different suggestions for cocktails on a chalkboard, as well as a mocktail for the drivers, to mix for themselves. Set out buckets of ice, slices of orange, lime and lemon, herbs like lemon verbena or lemon balm for decorating drinks, and straws and tall spoons in jars.

Seating plan or not? It's your preference (I prefer not), but try to steer chatty folks next to the slightly quieter ones.

Use vintage jars, little old teapots or jugs as flower vases and line them up along the table. Pretty fabric for tablecloths can look light and fresh.

As for the food, don't overcomplicate the menu. Serve two or three nibbles: one should be healthy and the other two indulgent. Choose a main course that's special and that you feel comfortable preparing. For a dinner party for six to eight, try beef fillet or a pan-fried sea bass with vegetables that tower to give height. Choose impressive desserts – either just one or a trio of mini ones if you feel adventurous. Serve coffee and a little something special to end with, like homemade chocolate, thin slices of fudge or hot chocolate stirrers. But most of all, relax and have fun!

30G BUTTER

2 ONIONS, FINELY DICED

1 GARLIC CLOVE, SLICED

1 CARROT, DICED

1 FENNEL BULB, DICED

1.5 LITRES FISH STOCK

125ML WHITE WINE

3 SAFFRON STRANDS, SOAKED IN 2 TBSP WATER

2 TBSP TOMATO PURÉE

½ TSP CHOPPED FRESH THYME

350G RAW PRAWNS, SHELLED AND DEVEINED,
 PLUS 8 PRAWNS WITH TAILS ON

SALT AND FRESHLY GROUND BLACK PEPPER

100ML CREAM

2 TBSP CHOPPED FRESH DILL, TO GARNISH

PRAWN AND FENNEL BISQUE

....

I love to serve this soup for a special occasion like Christmas or a dinner party for a friend's 'big zero' birthday, though we stopped counting our birthday numbers when we got to the upper 20s and now just enjoy the celebrations!

SERVES 4

1 Melt the butter in a large saucepan over a medium-low heat. Add the onions and sauté for 5–6 minutes, then add the garlic and cook for 1 minute more. Stir in the carrot and fennel and continue to cook for 4–5 minutes, stirring from time to time.

2 Pour in the fish stock, wine, the saffron and its soaking water, the tomato purée and the thyme and simmer over a low heat for 10 minutes. Transfer the soup to a blender and process until smooth, then return it to the saucepan. Stir in the 350g raw prawns and cook over a low heat for about 4 minutes. Check the seasoning. Stir in the cream and heat for 1 minute.

3 Place the remaining 8 prawns in a steamer set over boiling water and cook for about 4 minutes, until pink.

4 Ladle the soup into warm soup bowls. Place 2 cooked prawns in the centre of each bowl and sprinkle around a little fresh dill to garnish. Serve immediately.

4 LARGE ORANGES, PEELED AND SLICED
1 RED ONION, VERY THINLY SLICED
150G SOFT GOAT'S CHEESE
75G ROCKET, WASHED AND TRIMMED
2 TBSP PINE NUTS, TOASTED

FOR THE DRESSING:
100G RASPBERRIES
2 TBSP BALSAMIC VINEGAR
½ TSP WHOLEGRAIN MUSTARD
90ML EXTRA VIRGIN OLIVE OIL
SALT AND FRESHLY GROUND BLACK PEPPER

1 To prepare the dressing, place the raspberries, balsamic vinegar and mustard in a food processor and blend. While the motor is still running, pour in the oil in a thin stream and blend until smooth. Season to taste.

2 Arrange the oranges on 4 starter plates and place the onion slices and spoonfuls of goat's cheese on top. Sprinkle the rocket over and end with the pine nuts. Drizzle over the dressing and serve immediately.

ORANGE AND ROCKET SALAD WITH RASPBERRY VINAIGRETTE

....

This casual salad always looks fabulous on a slate or a slightly concave dark plate. But it isn't only the looks that we're going for – this freshens your palate with wonderful citrus flavours and is fairly healthy as well.

SERVES 4

350G SALMON, SKINNED, DEBONED AND CUT INTO 3CM PIECES
1 LEMON, THINLY SLICED
2 TBSP SUNFLOWER OIL
LIME WEDGES, TO SERVE

FOR THE MARINADE:
100ML SOY SAUCE
1 GARLIC CLOVE, FINELY CHOPPED
1 X 3CM PIECE OF FRESH GINGER, PEELED AND GRATED
ZEST AND JUICE OF 1 LEMON
2 TBSP HONEY
2 TSP SESAME OIL

FOR THE SALAD:
50G ASSORTED BABY SALAD LEAVES
50G ROCKET, WASHED AND TRIMMED
50G MANGETOUT, STEAMED
3 SPRING ONIONS, THINLY SLICED
1 CUCUMBER, SLICED INTO RIBBONS
DASH OF SESAME OIL
SQUEEZE OF LEMON JUICE
SALT AND FRESHLY GROUND BLACK PEPPER
2 TSP BLACK SESAME SEEDS

SESAME SALMON SKEWERS

....

If you can find micro greens like baby beetroot leaves, watercress or sprouts, the salmon skewers will pop with colour and the vivid brightness will wow your friends. The marinade also makes a tasty dipping sauce that you can use with scallops or prawns. I find that the salmon needs to be chunky or it won't stay on the skewers when chargrilling.

SERVES 4

1 If you're using bamboo skewers, soak 4 skewers in water for at least 2 hours.

2 Combine all the marinade ingredients in a large, shallow bowl. Add the salmon chunks to the marinade, making sure to coat all the fish. Cover the bowl with plastic wrap and place in the fridge for 15 minutes. Remove the marinated salmon from the fridge, shake off any excess marinade and thread the chunks onto the skewers, alternating with the lemon slices.

3 Brush the salmon skewers with the sunflower oil. Heat a griddle pan over a medium-high heat and sear the salmon for 1–2 minutes on each side. Keep an eye on them to make sure they don't overcook.

4 To serve, arrange the salad leaves, rocket, mangetout, spring onions and cucumber on 4 serving plates. Whisk together a dash of sesame oil, a squeeze of lemon juice and some salt and pepper, then drizzle over the salad. Place 1 salmon skewer on top of each plate, sprinkle with sesame seeds and serve with lime wedges.

TOMATO AND MOZZARELLA LAYERS WITH BASIL

· · · · · · · · · · · · · · · · · · ·

The crunch of the filo and the softness of the tomato and the mozzarella with a thin line of the green basil leaves gives this starter a real Italian feel, not only because of the ingredients, but because of the red, white and green colours too. Filo pastry isn't an everyday ingredient for me, but I find that it's helpful when I'm in a rush and want a delicate crispness. Just keep it damp by covering the sheets with a damp tea towel and be generous with the layers that you use, brushing with a mix of butter and olive oil.

SERVES 4

3 MEDIUM TOMATOES, CUT INTO 1CM-THICK SLICES
8 LARGE BASIL LEAVES, WASHED, PLUS EXTRA
  TO GARNISH
100G BUFFALO MOZZARELLA, CUT INTO
  1CM-THICK SLICES
SALT AND FRESHLY GROUND BLACK PEPPER
4 SHEETS OF FILO PASTRY
50G BUTTER, MELTED, FOR BRUSHING THE PASTRY
2 TBSP EXTRA VIRGIN OLIVE OIL

FOR THE BALSAMIC REDUCTION:
125ML BALSAMIC VINEGAR
1 TBSP HONEY

1 To make the balsamic vinegar reduction, pour the vinegar and honey into a small saucepan and simmer over a low heat for about 15 minutes, until reduced and sticky, stirring from time to time.

2 Preheat the oven to 180°C/fan 160°C/gas 4. Line a baking tray with parchment paper.

3 To assemble, make a tower by layering a slice of tomato, a basil leaf, a slice of mozzarella, a basil leaf and finishing with a slice of tomato on the top. Season with salt and freshly ground black pepper.

4 Cut each sheet of filo pastry into 4 long rectangles that are 8cm wide. Brush 1 rectangle of filo with melted butter and place another piece of filo on top. Repeat with the other rectangles. Place 2 pieces over each other to form a cross and place on the lined baking tray. Place a tomato tower in the centre and wrap the tower in the filo. Carefully twist the pastry tightly together and brush with melted butter. Bake for about 7 minutes, until the pastry is golden and crisp.

5 To serve, drizzle the extra virgin olive oil and balsamic vinegar reduction around each plate. Using a bread knife, cut the tower diagonally and place on the plate. Garnish with basil leaves and serve immediately.

50G WATERCRESS, WASHED

50G BABY SPINACH LEAVES, WASHED AND TRIMMED

2 LARGE SPRIGS FRESH FLAT-LEAF PARSLEY, LEAVES ONLY

½ CUCUMBER, DICED

CRABMEAT FROM 2 CRABS (OR 300G GOOD-QUALITY
   FROZEN CRABMEAT)

FRESH CHERVIL OR FLAT-LEAF PARSLEY, LEAVES ONLY, TO
   GARNISH

1 LEMON, VERY THINLY SLICED, TO GARNISH

FOR THE DRESSING:

JUICE AND ZEST OF 1 LEMON

1 X 2CM PIECE OF FRESH GINGER, PEELED AND GRATED

½ RED CHILLI, FINELY CHOPPED

1 TBSP CASTER SUGAR

1 LARGE MANGO, PEELED AND DICED

100ML WHITE WINE

4 TBSP RAPESEED OIL

3 TBSP WATER

SALT AND FRESHLY GROUND BLACK PEPPER

CRAB SALAD WITH MANGO GINGER DRESSING

If you have taken the time and gone to the expense to find fresh crab, don't mess with it too much – just enjoy the sheer indulgence of this wonderful food. The dressing is cooked, so prepare this ahead of time to give it a chance to cool. We hardly ever get wonderfully ripe mangos, but it doesn't really matter in this recipe, as they're poached and the gorgeous sweetness is released.

SERVES 4

1 To make the dressing, place the lemon juice and zest, ginger, chilli and sugar into a medium saucepan over a medium-low heat. Simmer until the sugar is dissolved, stirring from time to time. Add the diced mango, white wine, rapeseed oil and water and simmer for 3 minutes, until the mango is just softened. Check the seasoning – if you feel it's a little too sweet, add a pinch of salt and a little freshly ground black pepper. Set aside to cool completely.

2 To assemble the salad, mix together the watercress, spinach, parsley and cucumber in a bowl.

3 Arrange the salad on 4 plates. Divide the crabmeat into 4 portions. Place a round cutter carefully on top of the salad and spoon in the crabmeat, then gently remove the cutter. Spoon the dressing over the crab and salad and around the plate. Garnish with chervil or parsley leaves and lemon slices and serve immediately.

CELERIAC SOUP WITH LEMON GREMOLATA

....

2 TBSP EXTRA VIRGIN OLIVE OIL
1 ONION, FINELY CHOPPED
2 GARLIC CLOVES, SLICED
2 MEDIUM POTATOES, PEELED AND CUT INTO 2CM DICE
1 CELERIAC, PEELED AND CUT INTO 2CM DICE
1.2 LITRES VEGETABLE STOCK
1 TSP CHOPPED FRESH THYME
SALT AND FRESHLY GROUND BLACK PEPPER

FOR THE GREMOLATA:
1 GARLIC CLOVE, FINELY CHOPPED
ZEST OF 1 SMALL LEMON
3 TBSP CHOPPED FRESH PARSLEY
1 TSP CHOPPED FRESH DILL

This is a classic soup with a bit of a twist. It's nice to have a surprise every now and again, especially at a dinner party. A friend of mine always has wonderfully generous dinner parties. We had had a fabulous steak platter with all the trimmings. Then the main course was cleared and we had time to chat, when suddenly, an ice cream van arrived out of nowhere with our dessert (silly music and everything), and dessert wasn't just a '99', I can assure you! For a more low-key surprise, serve the gremolata on the soup spoons and everyone can sprinkle it over the soup themselves.

1 Heat the olive oil in a large saucepan over a medium heat. Add the onion and cook for 5 minutes, until softened but not brown. Add the garlic and cook for 1 minute more, stirring from time to time.

2 Add the potatoes and celeriac and cook for 2 minutes. Pour over the vegetable stock and thyme. Increase the heat and bring to the boil, then reduce the heat and simmer for 20 minutes, until the vegetables are tender. Blend the soup with a hand-held blender until smooth. Check for seasoning.

3 To make the gremolata, combine all the ingredients together in a small bowl and set aside.

4 To serve the soup, ladle it into a large tureen or warm soup bowls. Using a teaspoon, carefully sprinkle some gremolata in the centre of the soup and serve a small amount in a small bowl on the side. Serve immediately.

SERVES 4

ASPARAGUS AND STRAWBERRY SALAD WITH HONEY AND ORANGE DRESSING

....

All the components of this salad can be prepared ahead of time. Just before you're ready to serve, assemble the salad on a large serving platter and let your guests casually tuck in themselves, leaving you to enjoy a chat with everyone instead of plating up.

SERVES 4

12 ASPARAGUS SPEARS, TRIMMED

150G OF YOUR FAVOURITE LETTUCE LEAVES (OR TRY MIZUNA, COS, LITTLE GEM OR RED OAK), WASHED

8–10 LONG CHIVE STRANDS, WASHED AND TRIMMED

120G STRAWBERRIES, WASHED AND LEFT WHOLE OR SLICED

100G BLUE CHEESE, CRUMBLED

FOR THE DRESSING:

2 ORANGES (JUICE OF 2 AND ZEST OF 1)

100ML RAPESEED OIL

2 TBSP RED WINE VINEGAR

1 TBSP HONEY

1 TBSP FINELY CHOPPED CHIVES

SALT AND FRESHLY GROUND BLACK PEPPER

1 To prepare the dressing, mix together all the ingredients in a jar with a lid and shake well.

2 Place the asparagus in a steaming basket set over a saucepan of boiling water and steam for 4-5 minutes, until just tender. Once cooked, slice lengthways.

3 To assemble the salad, arrange the lettuce leaves, asparagus and chives on a platter. Scatter over the strawberries and crumble the blue cheese over the top. Drizzle over the dressing and serve immediately.

EXTRA VIRGIN OLIVE OIL

2 MEDIUM AUBERGINES, CUT INTO 1CM-THICK SLICES

2 GARLIC CLOVES, SLICED

SALT AND FRESHLY GROUND BLACK PEPPER

200G COOKED CHICKPEAS (TINNED ARE FINE)

4 BLACK OLIVES, SLICED

4 SUNDRIED TOMATO HALVES, ROUGHLY CHOPPED

1 TSP CHOPPED FRESH MARJORAM, PLUS EXTRA LEAVES
   TO GARNISH

1 TBSP RED WINE VINEGAR

½ TSP LIGHT BROWN SUGAR

100G FETA CHEESE, COARSELY CRUMBLED

AUBERGINE AND CHICKPEA MEDITER- RANEAN STACKS

....

1 Preheat the oven to 180°C /fan 160°C/gas 4.

2 Drizzle a little extra virgin olive oil in a large roasting pan and place it in the oven for a few minutes to heat the oil. Place the aubergine slices and garlic in the pan and drizzle a little more olive oil over the top. Season with salt and freshly ground black pepper and roast for 20-25 minutes, until soft. Set aside to cool.

3 Combine the chickpeas, olives, sundried tomatoes and marjoram together in a bowl. Stir in the vinegar and brown sugar.

4 To assemble the stack, place an aubergine disc into the base of a jar. Spoon in a layer of the chickpea and sundried tomato mixture, followed by an aubergine disc and then some crumbled feta cheese. Continue to layer up, ending with a little feta cheese. Drizzle over a very small amount of extra virgin olive oil, garnish with marjoram leaves and serve immediately.

This is a little different in that if looks great served in a jar, so start collecting them and your friends will be impressed! Just bear in mind that the aubergine disc has to fit into the base of the jar.

SERVES 4

8 ASPARAGUS SPEARS

4 X 150G SEA BASS FILLETS, SKIN ON

SALT AND FRESHLY GROUND BLACK PEPPER

SUNFLOWER OIL

2 PAK CHOI, TRIMMED AND ROUGHLY CHOPPED

1 X 2CM PIECE OF FRESH GINGER, PEELED AND SLICED
  INTO JULIENNE

2 TBSP SOY SAUCE

3 SPRING ONIONS, SLICED LENGTHWAYS

2 GARLIC CLOVES, THINLY SLICED

1 RED CHILLI, SLICED

2 TBSP SESAME SEEDS, TOASTED

1 Place the asparagus spears into a medium saucepan of boiling water and cook for 3 minutes. Remove from the saucepan and place into iced water. Drain and slice the asparagus lengthways.

2 Cut 3 incisions in the skin of each sea bass fillet, then season with salt and freshly ground black pepper. Heat some sunflower oil in a large frying pan over a medium heat. Add the fish, skin side down, and cook for about 4 minutes, until the skin is crisp and golden. Once crisp, carefully turn the fish over and cook for about 30 seconds. Place on a warm serving platter and cover with foil.

3 Meanwhile, heat a wok with a little sunflower oil over a high heat. Add the pak choi and stir-fry for about 2 minutes, until just tender. Add the ginger and soy sauce and stir-fry for 30 seconds, then add the asparagus and heat through. Add a little more oil to the pan and stir-fry the spring onions, garlic and red chilli for about 2 minutes.

4 Spoon the stir-fry onto a serving plate. Place the fish on top, spoon the sauce over the fish and sprinkle with sesame seeds. Serve immediately.

PAN-FRIED SEA BASS WITH CHILLI AND GINGER

....

The chilli and ginger combination is fabulous for sea bass, but you can use any fish, such as haddock or even monkfish, if you prefer.

SERVES 4

3–4 SPRIGS FRESH OREGANO, CHOPPED

2–3 SPRIGS FRESH THYME, CHOPPED

JUICE OF 1 LEMON

EXTRA VIRGIN OLIVE OIL

100G FETA, CRUMBLED

12 SMALL TO MEDIUM LAMB CUTLETS OR 8 LARGE
  CUTLETS, FRENCH TRIMMED

2 MEDIUM COURGETTES, SLICED LENGTHWAYS INTO
  RIBBONS

FRESH ROSEMARY SPRIGS, TO GARNISH

FRESH MINT SPRIGS, TO GARNISH

FOR THE TZATZIKI:

3 FRESH MINT LEAVES, FINELY CHOPPED

½ CUCUMBER, DICED

4 TBSP NATURAL YOGHURT

SALT AND FRESHLY GROUND BLACK PEPPER

LAMB CUTLETS WITH TZATZIKI

*Oregano grows very success-
fully in our herb garden here
at the cookery school, as does
thyme. These cutlets grill
fabulously on the BBQ. Serve
them with a panzanella salad.*

SERVES 4

1 Mix together the oregano and thyme with the lemon juice and 2 tablespoons of olive oil. Mix 2 teaspoons of this herby oil with the feta cheese and spread the rest over the lamb cutlets.

2 Heat a chargrill pan. Brush the courgette ribbons with olive oil on both sides. Once the pan is hot, place the courgettes in the pan and cook for about 1 minute on each side. Set aside and keep warm.

3 Place the cutlets in the hot chargrill pan and cook for 3–4 minutes on each side, depending on how you like them.

4 Combine all the ingredients for the tzatziki in a small bowl.

5 Divide the courgette ribbons between 4 plates and arrange 2 or 3 cutlets upright on the ribbons. Spoon over some feta cheese and the tzatziki and garnish with the sprigs of rosemary and mint.

4 MEDIUM DUCK BREASTS, TRIMMED
1 TSP GROUND CUMIN
½ TSP GROUND GINGER
2 ORANGES, THINLY SLICED, TO GARNISH
SUNFLOWER OIL
2 LEEKS, WASHED WELL AND SLICED LENGTHWAYS
½ SAVOY CABBAGE, LEAVES WASHED AND TRIMMED
SALT AND FRESHLY GROUND BLACK PEPPER

FOR THE SAUCE:
30G BUTTER
1 RED CHILLI, FINELY CHOPPED
½ TSP GRATED FRESH GINGER
100ML ORANGE JUICE

1 Preheat the oven to 200°C/fan 180°C/gas 6.

2 Make 3 long incisions in the skin of each duck breast, then rub with the cumin and ginger. Heat an ovenproof frying pan until very hot. Place the duck in the pan, skin side down, and cook for 3–4 minutes, until golden. Turn over and cook for 2 minutes.

3 Move the frying pan to the oven and cook for 8 minutes. Check for doneness and allow to rest for 5 minutes.

4 Meanwhile, to make the sauce, melt the butter in a small saucepan over a medium-low heat. Add the chilli and grated ginger and sauté for 2 minutes. Pour in the orange juice and cook for 3 minutes, until the chilli is softened and the sauce has slightly thickened. Set aside.

5 Heat a chargrill pan over a medium heat. Brush the orange slices with a little sunflower oil and chargrill the oranges on both sides.

6 Heat a little oil in a medium frying pan and sauté the sliced leeks for about 2 minutes, until just tender. Add the cabbage leaves and 2 tablespoons of water to the pan and toss the cabbage until it's just wilted and tender, which should take about 2 minutes. Season the vegetables with a little salt and freshly ground black pepper.

7 When ready to serve, heat the sauce. Using tongs, lift the leeks and cabbage onto a serving plate. Place the duck breasts on a board and carve diagonally into medium-thick slices. Place the sliced duck on top of the vegetables and spoon over the orange ginger sauce. Place the orange slices on top and serve immediately.

DUCK WITH ORANGE GINGER SAUCE

....

We have gone way past the days of tinned cherries around a duck at a dinner party. Try some other options, like roasted rhubarb and star anise or blackberries with cumin to serve with the slices of duck.

SERVES 4

600G VENISON FILLET
SUNFLOWER OIL
SALT AND FRESHLY GROUND BLACK PEPPER
15G BUTTER
20 RAW PRAWNS, SHELLED AND DEVEINED, TAILS LEFT ON
JUICE AND ZEST OF ½ LEMON
50ML DOUBLE CREAM
1 TBSP CHOPPED FRESH PARSLEY
50G WATERCRESS, WASHED
1 LEMON, SLICED INTO WEDGES

VENISON SURF AND TURF

······················

This surf and turf is a bit different, but it works very well. The 'surf' is delicious with venison, but when venison isn't in season, the classic beef fillet will do. Serve with the lemon salt roast potatoes on page 193.

SERVES 4

1 To prepare the venison, trim away any sinew that runs down the length of the fillet with a sharp knife. Brush the venison with a little sunflower oil and season with salt and freshly ground black pepper. Heat 2 tablespoons of oil and the butter in a large frying pan over a high heat and sear the fillet on all sides, until golden. Reduce the heat and gently cook the fillet, turning regularly, for 6–8 minutes, or until cooked to your liking. Transfer the venison to a warm plate and allow to rest.

2 Heat 1 tablespoon of the oil in a large frying pan over a medium heat. Add the prawns and sauté for about 2 minutes. Add in the lemon juice and zest and stir in the double cream. Check the seasoning, then add the parsley.

3 To serve, slice the venison into 4 thick slices and place each slice on a serving plate. Arrange prawns in between, spoon over the sauce and place some watercress on the side. Serve with lemon wedges.

800G BEEF FILLET, TRIMMED

EXTRA VIRGIN OLIVE OIL

TAMARIND AND HONEY ROASTED TURNIP, BEETROOT AND
 CARROT WEDGES (PAGE 126), TO SERVE

FOR THE SPICE RUB:

1 TSP GROUND GINGER

1 TSP TURMERIC

1 TSP FRESHLY GROUND BLACK PEPPER

½ TSP SALT

¼ TSP FRESHLY GRATED NUTMEG

1 Combine all the spice rub ingredients together in a small bowl.
Heat a small frying pan over a medium-low heat. Add the dry
spices and heat for 30 seconds, stirring all the time so the spices
don't burn. Allow the spices to cool, then rub them over the beef
fillet. Place the beef on a sheet of parchment paper, wrap it up
in the paper and then cover with plastic wrap. Place in the fridge
to allow the flavours to infuse for at least 5 hours, or preferably
overnight.

2 Take the beef out of the fridge 30 minutes before you're ready to
cook it. Preheat the oven to 190°C/fan 170°C/gas 5.

3 Heat some oil in a large frying pan over a high heat. Sear the fillet
for 2-3 minutes on each side to colour. Using tongs, transfer to a
roasting pan.

4 Roast the beef for 20-22 minutes for rare, 26-30 minutes for
medium or 35-40 minutes for well done. Allow to stand for 10
minutes before carving. Serve with the tamarind and honey roasted
turnips, beetroot and carrot wedges.

MOROCCAN-STYLE BEEF FILLET

....

*These Moroccan flavours are
warm and inviting. The spices
will certainly be in your store
cupboard, and once blended
you can keep them sealed in
a jar for a few weeks. I love to
use whole nutmeg and grate it
freshly into the spice mix.*

SERVES 4

EXTRA VIRGIN OLIVE OIL

2 TBSP HONEY

2 TSP CHOPPED FRESH ROSEMARY

2 X 200G LEAN LEG OF LAMB STEAKS

16 VINE-RIPENED CHERRY TOMATOES, WASHED AND
LEFT WHOLE

2 GARLIC CLOVES, ROUGHLY SLICED

ZEST OF 1 ORANGE

SALT AND FRESHLY GROUND BLACK PEPPER

CHARGRILLED LAMB SALAD WITH LEMON DRESSING

....

The juicy pink slices of chargrilled lamb lie in between the layers of garden leaves, tomatoes and crunchy croutons for a casual party main course that everyone will enjoy.

SERVES 4

FOR THE HERB CROUTONS:

200G STALE WHITE BREAD

EXTRA VIRGIN OLIVE OIL

HANDFUL OF FRESH HERBS (CHIVES, ROSEMARY AND/
OR THYME), CHOPPED

SALT AND FRESHLY GROUND BLACK PEPPER

FOR THE SALAD:

120G GARDEN SALAD LEAVES

4 SMALL SPRIGS OF FRESH ROSEMARY

FOR THE LEMON DRESSING:

ZEST AND JUICE OF 1 LEMON

6 TBSP EXTRA VIRGIN OLIVE OIL

1 TSP WHOLEGRAIN MUSTARD

1 TSP HONEY

SALT AND FRESHLY GROUND BLACK PEPPER

1 Preheat the oven to 180°C/fan 160°C/gas 4.

2 Combine 3 tablespoons of extra virgin olive oil with the honey and chopped rosemary in a bowl. Brush over the lamb steaks and allow to infuse for 40 minutes to 1 hour.

3 Meanwhile, to make the croutons, tear up the stale bread into bite-sized pieces and place on a baking tray, then drizzle with extra virgin olive oil, scatter over a good handful of chopped herbs and season with salt and pepper. Toss together and toast in the oven for about 20 minutes, shaking the pan from time to time.

4 Place the tomatoes, garlic and orange zest in a roasting tin and drizzle with some extra virgin olive oil. Roast for about 20 minutes, then season with salt and freshly ground black pepper.

5 Whisk together all the lemon dressing ingredients.

6 Heat a chargrill pan over a medium heat. Place the lamb steaks in the pan and sear on all sides. Transfer to a roasting tin and cook for about 8 minutes, until the lamb is cooked but just pink. Place on a warm plate, cover and allow the lamb to rest for 5–6 minutes before slicing.

7 To serve, place the salad leaves on a serving platter. Arrange the rosemary sprigs, roasted tomatoes and garlic over the salad leaves, then add the sliced lamb. Spoon over some lemon dressing and then sprinkle the croutons on top and enjoy.

TIAN OF BALLY-KNOCKEN VEGETABLES

....

15G BUTTER, MELTED

3 GARLIC CLOVES, SLICED

2 MEDIUM LEEKS, WASHED, TRIMMED AND SLICED

2 COURGETTES, SLICED

2 MEDIUM POTATOES, THINLY SLICED

2 MEDIUM TOMATOES, SLICED

1 TSP CHOPPED FRESH THYME, PLUS FRESH SPRIGS
   TO GARNISH

100ML WHITE WINE

EXTRA VIRGIN OLIVE OIL

SALT AND FRESHLY GROUND BLACK PEPPER

A tian has colourful layers sitting vertically in a dish, and the vegetable tians are the most popular. I like to use vegetables from our patch here at the cookery school. I can't claim too much fame for growing tomatoes – last season our greenhouse was blown down in a strong wind and found in the field next door – but we always have a good crop of courgettes, potatoes, leeks and even garlic.

SERVES 4

1 Preheat the oven to 180°C/fan 160°C/gas 4. Brush a 20cm square, oval or circular shallow casserole with the melted butter.

2 Layer all the sliced vegetables in a row, starting from the outside and standing them upright in the casserole. Sprinkle over the chopped thyme and pour over the white wine with a drizzle of olive oil. Sprinkle over a little salt and freshly ground black pepper. Cover with a piece of foil and bake for 20 minutes, then remove the foil and continue to bake for 20 minutes more.

3 Scatter over the sprigs of thyme. Allow to cool slightly before serving, as the tomatoes will be extremely hot.

TAMARIND AND HONEY ROASTED TURNIP, BEETROOT AND CARROT WEDGES

....

The citrus flavour of the tamarind teamed with honey over these roasted vegetables is tasty and colourful. An extra bonus is that they can be prepared ahead of time. Serve them with the Moroccan-style beef fillet on page 121. If you have any leftover vegetables, add some stock and blend them to form a chunky winter soup.

SERVES 4

4 CARROTS, PEELED AND CUT INTO WEDGES
4 GARLIC CLOVES, SLICED
2 TURNIPS, PEELED AND CUT INTO THIN WEDGES
2 MEDIUM BEETROOTS, PEELED AND CUT INTO WEDGES
1 TBSP ROUGHLY CHOPPED FRESH CORIANDER, TO GARNISH

FOR THE TAMARIND DRIZZLE:
4 TBSP EXTRA VIRGIN OLIVE OIL
2 TBSP HONEY
1 TSP TAMARIND PASTE
SALT AND FRESHLY GROUND BLACK PEPPER

1 Preheat the oven to 180°C/fan 160°C/gas 4. Line a roasting tin with parchment paper.

2 Mix all the ingredients for the tamarind drizzle together in a large bowl. Toss the vegetables in the tamarind mixture and then spoon into the roasting tin and drizzle with a little olive oil.

3 Roast for 25–30 minutes, until the vegetables are cooked through. Transfer to a warm serving bowl and sprinkle over the chopped coriander.

CHARGRILLED RED PEPPER AND AUBERGINE SKEWERS

Skewers for a dinner party? Aren't they just for BBQs? These are great for dinner parties, as the dish is already portioned, so you don't have to worry that you won't have enough vegetables for everyone.

MAKES 4

3 TBSP SUNFLOWER OIL, PLUS EXTRA FOR BRUSHING

2 TSP PAPRIKA

1 TSP CHOPPED FRESH OREGANO

1 TSP LIGHT BROWN SUGAR

JUICE OF 1 LEMON

1 AUBERGINE, THINLY SLICED LENGTHWAYS, THEN EACH SLICED INTO 3 STRIPS

1 RED PEPPER, ROUGHLY DICED

SALT AND FRESHLY GROUND BLACK PEPPER

1 Soak 4 bamboo skewers in water for at least 2 hours.

2 Combine the oil, paprika, oregano, brown sugar and lemon juice in a large, shallow bowl. Add in the aubergine and red pepper and marinate for 30 minutes.

3 Thread the aubergine strips and red peppers onto the skewers, then brush with sunflower oil. Sprinkle with salt and freshly ground black pepper.

4 Heat a chargrill pan over a medium heat and cook the skewers for about 5 minutes in total, turning the skewers occasionally, until the aubergine is cooked. Place the skewers on a platter and serve.

250G FRENCH BEANS, TRIMMED
1 TBSP EXTRA VIRGIN OLIVE OIL
1 RED ONION, FINELY SLICED
2 GARLIC CLOVES, THINLY SLICED
12 WALNUT HALVES, ROUGHLY CHOPPED

1 Place the green beans in a steamer over a medium heat and cook for about 4 minutes, until just tender.

2 Meanwhile, heat the olive oil in a frying pan over a medium heat. Add the onion and sauté for 4–5 minutes, until softened but not brown. Add in the garlic and cook for 1 minute more.

3 Toss the beans and walnuts into the frying pan and cook for 1–2 minutes. Spoon into a warm serving bowl and serve immediately.

GARLIC FRENCH BEANS WITH WALNUTS

....

I love the crunchiness of the walnuts and the crisp freshness of French beans. If you have someone in the party who has a nut allergy, replace the walnuts with orange zest and crumble soft goat's cheese on top.

SERVES 4

8 LARGE FLOURY POTATOES, PEELED AND CUT IN HALF
5 TBSP EXTRA VIRGIN OLIVE OIL
¼ TSP CHILLI FLAKES (EVEN A PINCH WILL DO)
2½ TSP CHOPPED FRESH ROSEMARY
SEA SALT AND FRESHLY GROUND BLACK PEPPER

1 Preheat the oven to 220°C/fan 200°C/gas 7.

2 Steam the potatoes for about 12 minutes.

3 Pour the extra virgin olive oil into a roasting tin and heat in the oven. Toss the potatoes, chilli flakes and 1 ½ teaspoons of the chopped rosemary into the tin along with some salt and pepper. Roast for 30–35 minutes, until the potatoes are crispy on the outside and soft inside. Turn the potatoes after 15 minutes to ensure they get crispy all over. Once cooked, sprinkle over the remaining teaspoon of chopped rosemary and toss.

CHILLI AND ROSEMARY ROAST POTATOES

....

You can never have enough potatoes at a party. I would say serving 3 to 4 small potatoes is average, but for my family I always prepare more. They are the nation's favourite, after all! Try making these using goose fat – they're delicious.

SERVES 4

FOR THE CARAMEL MOUSSE:
3 TBSP CASTER SUGAR

1 TBSP ESPRESSO COFFEE

150ML DOUBLE CREAM

60G MILK CHOCOLATE, CHOPPED

2 EGG YOLKS

1 TBSP ICING SUGAR

FOR THE WHITE CHOCOLATE MOUSSE:
175ML CREAM

1 GELATINE LEAF

100G WHITE CHOCOLATE DROPS

FOR THE CHOCOLATE SAUCE:
100G DARK CHOCOLATE (AT LEAST 70% COCOA SOLIDS)

60ML DOUBLE CREAM

1 To make the caramel mousse, place the caster sugar and 2 table-spoons of water in a small saucepan over a medium-low heat and carefully swirl it (don't stir it!) until it caramelises. Remove from the heat and add the espresso and 50ml of the double cream, taking care as it will bubble up. Stir until the sugar dissolves. Place the chocolate into a large bowl and pour the hot caramel cream over the chocolate, stirring until it melts. Allow to cool slightly, then whisk in the egg yolks until smooth.

2 Pour the remaining 100ml double cream into a separate bowl. Add the icing sugar and whisk until soft peaks form, then fold the whipped cream into the chocolate and caramel. Spoon the mousse into pretty serving glasses until each glass is one-third full. Place in the fridge for about 1 hour, until chilled and just set.

3 Meanwhile, to make the white chocolate mousse, heat 100ml of the cream over a medium heat until just simmering, then remove from the heat. Soak the gelatine leaf in a shallow bowl of cold water until just soft, then squeeze out the excess water and add to the hot cream, stirring until smooth. Place the white chocolate into a bowl, pour over the warm cream and stir until melted and smooth. Allow to cool to room temperature. Whisk the remaining 75ml cream into soft peaks, then carefully fold into the cooled white chocolate mixture.

4 Take the caramel mousse out of the fridge and spoon the white chocolate mousse into the glasses until each glass is now two-thirds full. Return to the fridge for about 30 minutes.

5 To make the chocolate sauce, place the chocolate and cream in a small saucepan and melt over a low heat, stirring all the time. Allow to cool, then spoon the sauce over the white chocolate mousse and chill in the fridge for 20 minutes, or until you're ready to serve.

WICKED MOUSSE LAYERS

....

Just like the title says, this is a very rich dessert to end a meal. You will only need a little, so serve them in small glasses. It's not for anyone counting the calories, but relax, it's the weekend – you can diet during the week!

MAKES 2 LARGE (SO YOU CAN SHARE), 4 MEDIUM OR 6 SMALL GLASSES

BUTTERMILK PANNA COTTA WITH SPICY PINEAPPLE

········

There are a few recipes that I can't resist adding to cooking classes or including in my books, and versions of panna cotta is one of them. Using the buttermilk still adds the creaminess and smoothness but keeps it zingy. This one is for those busy times when you want something mouth-watering to prepare ahead.

MAKES 4

FOR THE PANNA COTTA:
80G CASTER SUGAR
200ML DOUBLE CREAM
½ TSP VANILLA EXTRACT
2 GELATINE LEAVES
230ML BUTTERMILK

FOR THE SPICY PINEAPPLE:
15G BUTTER
½ PINEAPPLE, PEELED AND NEATLY DICED
125G CASTER SUGAR
½ TSP GROUND CUMIN
¼ TSP CHILLI POWDER

1 To make the panna cotta, place the sugar, double cream and vanilla extract into a medium saucepan over a medium heat to dissolve the sugar, stirring all the time. Once dissolved, remove from the heat.

2 Meanwhile, soak the gelatine in about 100ml cold water, until softened. Squeeze out the excess water from the gelatine and add to the hot cream and stir until the gelatine dissolves. Carefully stir in the buttermilk and then pour into a jug.

3 Place 8 dariole moulds or ramekins on a tray and pour in the mixture. Place in the fridge to set for at least 5 hours.

4 To make the spicy pineapple, melt the butter in a medium non-stick saucepan over a medium heat. Add the diced pineapple, sugar, cumin and chilli powder and gently sauté for about 15 minutes, stirring from time to time. (Do not use an aluminium pan, as it will react with the pineapple.) Set aside to cool.

5 To serve, unmould the panna cotta by dipping the moulds in hot water for a few seconds, then place a serving plate on top, tip it over and carefully lift off the mould. Spoon the spicy pineapple on top of the panna cotta and serve immediately.

FOR THE ICE CREAM:

200G GOLDEN CASTER SUGAR

3 EGG YOLKS

600ML DOUBLE CREAM

2 TBSP MATCHA GREEN TEA POWDER (AVAILABLE IN
   ASIAN SHOPS)

FOR THE PISTACHIO SHARDS:

180G CASTER SUGAR

3 TBSP PISTACHIO NUTS, ROUGHLY CHOPPED

1 To make the ice cream, whisk the sugar and egg yolks together in a large bowl until pale and thick. Heat the cream in a saucepan over a medium heat, but do not boil. Pour the cream into the sugar and egg yolks, then pour everything back into the saucepan. Cook over a low heat, whisking all the time, until a thick custard forms, taking care that it doesn't scramble. Add the matcha green tea powder and whisk well. Pour into an ice cream maker and chill according to the manufacturer's instructions or transfer into a plastic container and freeze for 4–5 hours, until firm.

2 To make the pistachio shards, line a baking sheet with parchment paper. Heat the sugar in a saucepan over a medium heat, carefully swirling from time to time (don't stir it!), until golden. Remove from the heat and add the pistachios to the light caramel. Pour the caramel onto the lined baking sheet, spreading thinly. Once it has hardened, crack into pieces.

3 To serve, spoon the ice cream into small bowls, add a pistachio shard on top and serve immediately.

GREEN TEA ICE CREAM WITH PISTACHIO SHARDS

....

This will hit the spot. Serve the ice cream in mini homemade tuile cones and stand in shot glasses with blackberries infused in cassis and a bowl of finely chopped hazelnuts for guests to dunk their ice cream into the nuts for some fun.

SERVES 4-6

FOR THE RASPBERRY COULIS:
250G RASPBERRIES
2–3 TBSP CASTER SUGAR
2 TBSP WATER

FOR THE FILLING:
100G WHITE CHOCOLATE
150G MASCARPONE
200ML CREAM
ZEST OF 2 LEMONS
3 TBSP ICING SUGAR
150G RASPBERRIES, PLUS A FEW EXTRA TO DECORATE
1 X 400G MADEIRA CAKE, THINLY SLICED
12 WALNUTS, ROUGHLY CHOPPED
4–5 TBSP NOCINO (WALNUT) LIQUEUR, GRAPPA OR
  SWEET WINE

1 Oil a 900g loaf tin and line with plastic wrap.

2 To make the coulis, place the raspberries, sugar and water in a blender and whizz until smooth. Press through a sieve to remove the seeds.

3 To make the filling, melt the chocolate in a bowl set over a saucepan of simmering water (bain marie). Remove the bowl of chocolate from the heat and allow it to cool slightly, then carefully mix with the mascarpone.

4 Lightly whip the chocolate mascarpone, cream, lemon zest and icing sugar together in a large bowl.

5 Cover the base of the loaf tin with a layer of raspberries. Spoon over the chocolate cream, then add a layer of Madeira cake slices. Sprinkle over some walnuts and drizzle over the nocino. Continue layering, ending with the chocolate cream.

6 Cover with plastic wrap and leave in the fridge for at least 24 hours.

7 To serve, unmould the terrine onto a serving platter, pour over the raspberry coulis and decorate the top with a few fresh raspberries.

RASPBERRY AND LEMON TERRINE

....

Catering for a large party is a hard task, but this dessert is a winner. It's easy to slice and can be prepared 2 days ahead of time, as you want all the flavours to develop. It's a bit like a trifle loaf, actually – a very delicious trifle loaf! At Christmas I often make this with Pandora cake.

SERVES 6-8 (MAKES 1 X 900G LOAF)

FOR THE BISCUIT BASE:
120G UNSALTED BUTTER, MELTED AND SLIGHTLY COOLED
200G AMARETTI BISCUITS

FOR THE FILLING:
600ML DOUBLE CREAM
ZEST OF 1 ORANGE
PULP OF 2 PASSION FRUIT
100G GREEK YOGHURT
1 TSP VANILLA EXTRACT
120G STRAWBERRIES, WASHED AND SLICED
  INTO QUARTERS

NO BAKE STRAWBERRY AND ORANGE TARTLETS

....

A 'no bake' dessert takes the pressure off in that last-minute rush before guests arrive. The Greek yoghurt balances the sweetness here and soothes the sharpness of the passion fruit.

1 Brush 6 x 10cm loose-bottomed, fluted tartlet tins (or 1 x 24cm loose-bottomed, fluted tart tin) with a little of the melted butter.

2 Place the amaretti biscuits in a food processor and whizz until they're fine crumbs. Add the butter and pulse a few times to combine, then carefully press the crumbs into the base and sides of the tartlet tins. Place in the fridge to set for 30 minutes.

3 To make the filling, whisk the cream and orange zest in a large mixing bowl with an electric beater until stiff peaks form. Add the passion fruit pulp and stir to combine. Fold in the yoghurt and vanilla extract until mixed through.

4 Spoon the filling into the set biscuit bases and chill again for 3 hours. When ready to serve, arrange the strawberries around the edge of the tartlets.

**MAKES 6 X 10CM TARTLETS
OR 1 X 24CM TART**

FOR THE SEMIFREDDO:
100G GOLDEN CASTER SUGAR
4 LARGE EGGS
220G DARK CHOCOLATE DROPS
500ML DOUBLE CREAM, WHIPPED TO STIFF PEAKS

FOR THE PISTACHIOS:
120G CASTER SUGAR
1 TBSP WATER
100G UNSALTED, SHELLED PISTACHIO NUTS

RASPBERRIES, BLUEBERRIES, BLACKBERRIES OR
   REDCURRANTS, TO DECORATE

CHOCOLATE SEMIFREDDO WITH PISTACHIOS AND BERRIES

This will take a little more time than usual to complete but it's well worth it. This is a slightly soft, delicate semi-freddo. Choose small freezer moulds, as it's very rich. Just give yourself plenty of time to freeze it. Serve with pistachios and seasonal berries for a very glamorous affair.

SERVES 6 (USING 6CM–8CM MOULDS OR RAMEKINS)

1 Line 6 dariole moulds or ramekins with plastic wrap and place in the freezer to chill.

2 Fill a medium saucepan with a little water and bring to the boil, then reduce the heat to a simmer. Place a heatproof bowl over the saucepan, making sure that the water does not touch the bowl. Add the sugar and eggs and whisk with an electric beater until pale, thick and doubled in volume. Remove the bowl from the saucepan, plunge the base into cold water and whisk until the mixture is cool.

3 Melt the chocolate drops in a heatproof bowl set over the saucepan of simmering water, stirring from time to time. Remove the bowl from the saucepan and carefully fold the chocolate into the cooled egg mixture, then fold in the whipped cream. Ladle the semifreddo into the chilled moulds and cover the top with plastic wrap. Freeze overnight, until firm.

4 To prepare the pistachios, line a baking tray with parchment paper. Add the sugar and water to a small saucepan set over a medium heat, swirling (not stirring!) every so often until lightly caramelised. Place the pistachios on the parchment and carefully pour the caramel over the nuts. Allow to cool, then crack the caramel pistachios into 3cm uneven pieces.

5 To serve, unmould the semifreddo by dipping the base of the moulds into some hot water. Place on a serving platter and remove the plastic wrap. Scatter some berries over the semifreddo and arrange the caramel pistachios on top. Serve immediately.

SAFFRON MERINGUES WITH ORANGE CREAM

MAKES 24 X 3CM MERINGUES

These have a pale creamy pink tinge to them and a delicate, slightly Middle Eastern flavour. They also take on a brighter colour when baked, so don't be lashing in the saffron (which is too expensive anyway to be lashing in!). You could omit the saffron and use 1 teaspoon of vanilla extract or rosewater instead.

FOR THE MERINGUES:
12 (A PINCH) SAFFRON STRANDS
6 EGG WHITES
360G CASTER SUGAR
1 TSP CORNFLOUR
1 TSP WHITE WINE VINEGAR

FOR THE ORANGE CREAM:
350ML CREAM
ZEST OF 2 ORANGES
2 TBSP ICING SUGAR

1 Preheat the oven to 120°C/fan 100°C/gas 1. Line 2 baking trays with parchment paper.

2 Soak the saffron in 2 tablespoons of lukewarm water for 15 minutes.

3 Whisk the egg whites in a clean, dry bowl until stiff. Gradually add half the sugar a spoonful at a time, whisking after each addition, then fold in the rest. Continue whisking until the meringue is thick and glossy. Fold in the cornflour, white wine vinegar and the saffron and its soaking liquid.

4 Spoon the meringue into a piping bag and pipe 3cm circles onto the parchment paper, swirling upwards to form pretty peaks. Bake for 1 hour, then turn the oven off and leave the meringues to cool in the oven (which will take about 1 hour but overnight is fine).

5 To make the orange cream, whip the cream until soft peaks form. Fold in the orange zest and icing sugar and chill before serving.

6 Set out the meringues and cream separately for a DIY dessert bar, or to make individual portions, sandwich 2 meringues together with a dollop of cream.

DIY DESSERT BAR

I saw this at a wedding and it makes perfect sense to have a DIY dessert bar for everyone to enjoy creating their own yummy designs. Have plenty of long-handled spoons for serving. I like the saffron meringues to be slightly marshmallowy inside and crispy outside. The chocolate drizzle is smooth with a hint of spiciness and so easy to make, as is the orange cream. The lime curd is 'Ms Make Ahead of Time' and can be prepared a few weeks in advance, while the sesame pastry cases are delicate and melt in your mouth. Everything is inter-changeable and guests can choose their own combination to make everyone happy.

THIS WOULD EASILY SATISFY
ABOUT 10 GUESTS

CINNAMON CHOCOLATE DRIZZLE

MAKES ABOUT 400ML

This couldn't be easier. Spread it over a cake as a ganache and let it set before decorating it for a special birthday. You can also freeze the drizzle for a few weeks. Macadamia nuts could be added to the warm sauce as well.

200G CHOCOLATE DROPS
250ML DOUBLE CREAM
½ TSP GROUND CINNAMON (OR TO TASTE)

1 Combine all the ingredients in a medium saucepan and melt over a low heat, stirring most of the time. Pour into a bowl or jug and serve warm.

SESAME PASTRY CASES

MAKES 24 HEART SHAPES

Try to roll the pastry out very thinly between 2 pieces of plastic wrap, as it can be difficult, and allow it to rest a little. Once you have shaped the cases, put the baking tray back in the fridge to chill for 20 minutes before baking.

MELTED BUTTER, FOR GREASING
220G PLAIN FLOUR, PLUS EXTRA FOR DUSTING
2 TBSP SESAME SEEDS, PLUS EXTRA FOR SPRINKLING
100G CHILLED BUTTER, DICED
1 EGG, BEATEN
1 EGG YOLK, BEATEN
1 EGG MIXED WITH 2 TBSP WATER, FOR EGG WASH

1 Brush 2 x 12-hole shallow, non-stick tartlet baking trays with melted butter and dust with flour.

2 Mix the flour and 2 tablespoons of the sesame seeds in a large bowl. Rub in the chilled butter with your fingertips until it resembles fine breadcrumbs. Mix together the egg and the egg yolk, then add just enough egg to bind the pastry and form a soft ball. Roll up and wrap in cling film and leave to rest in the fridge for 20 minutes.

3 Dust a work surface with flour and roll out the pastry until it's 5mm thick. Cut out 24 heart shapes and lift them into the tins. Carefully prick the base with a fork, taking care not to pierce all the way through. Brush with egg wash and sprinkle a few sesame seeds on top. Allow to rest for about 20 minutes in the fridge.

4 Preheat the oven to 190°C/fan 170°C/gas 5.

5 Bake for 6–8 minutes, until golden and crisp. Allow to cool in the baking trays. Remove from the trays and pile up in a jar or pretty bowl, ready to be filled.

100G GOLDEN CASTER SUGAR
30G UNSALTED BUTTER, DICED
2 EGGS, LIGHTLY BEATEN
2 LIMES (JUICE OF 2 AND ZEST OF 1)

1 Put the sugar, butter, eggs and lime juice in a heavy-based saucepan and simmer over a moderately low heat, whisking until it's thick enough to hold marks from the whisk. This will take 12–15 minutes.

2 Immediately pour the curd through a sieve into a bowl. Stir in the zest of 1 lime and allow to cool before pouring into a pretty jar. The lime curd can be made up to 1 week in advance – just cover the surface with cling film and seal. Once open, store in the fridge.

LIME CURD

MAKES ABOUT 120ML

This lime curd completes this celebration of desserts. It just screams 'eat me, I'm delicious', not only as a pie filling but over ginger scones, as a topping for panna cotta, over slices of fresh melon or just as a gift for your friends and neighbours.

STRAWBERRY AND ORANGE SODAS

....

Prepare stock syrup and leave it in the fridge, ready for your new drink inventions. Collect some classic glasses to serve your drinks in – the tall and elegant ones will be very useful. Pop straws, pretty ice shapes and fruit slices into the glasses and enjoy. Add a dash of vodka and serve as a welcome cocktail.

MAKES 800ML

250G CASTER SUGAR

500ML WATER

250G STRAWBERRIES, WASHED AND HULLED, PLUS A FEW EXTRA TO GARNISH

2 TBSP ICING SUGAR

125ML ORANGE JUICE

ZEST OF 1 ORANGE

500ML SPARKLING WATER

ORANGE SLICES, TO GARNISH

1 Combine the sugar and water in a saucepan over a medium heat. Bring to the boil, then reduce the heat and simmer for about 15 minutes, until a syrup has formed. Allow to cool.

2 Add the strawberries and icing sugar to a food processor and blend until smooth, then mix with the orange juice and zest and the syrup. Quarter-fill 4 tall glasses with the strawberry and orange purée and then top up with sparkling water. Garnish with strawberries and orange slices.

WATERMELON MOJITOS

....

A great tipple to start the evening off. Write the recipe on a chalkboard for everyone to prepare for themselves or serve them at the start of the evening on a pretty tray.

MAKES 5-6

600G WATERMELON, PEELED, SEEDS REMOVED AND DICED

20 FRESH MINT LEAVES, PLUS EXTRA TO GARNISH

JUICE OF 4 LIMES

200ML WHITE RUM

4 TBSP CASTER SUGAR

CRUSHED ICE, TO SERVE

1 Place the watermelon, mint leaves, lime juice, rum and sugar in a blender and process until smooth. Pour into glasses over crushed ice and garnish with sprigs of mint.

POMEGRANATE SPARKLER

....

500ML POMEGRANATE JUICE
1 TSP VANILLA EXTRACT
SEEDS FROM 1 POMEGRANATE, TO GARNISH
1 BOTTLE SPARKLING WINE, CHILLED
1 VANILLA POD FOR EACH GLASS (OPTIONAL)

1 Mix the pomegranate juice and vanilla extract together
and half-fill the champagne flutes. Add about 2 teaspoons of
pomegranate seeds to each flute and carefully top up with the
sparkling wine. Slide in the vanilla pod if you're using it.

*This is my favourite drink at
a Christmas dinner party, but
you can celebrate all year
round with this elegant spar-
kler. I wouldn't change a thing
here except to perhaps drink a
little more pomegranate juice
for its great vitamin C value!*
MAKES 6-8

(EASY LIKE)
SUNDAY
MORNING

'EASY LIKE SUNDAY MORNING' – THE COMMODORES

'HOW D'YA LIKE YOUR EGGS IN THE MORNING?'
– DEAN MARTIN AND HELEN O'CONNELL

'GOOD MORNING' (FROM *SINGIN' IN THE RAIN*)

CHAPTER 10

SUNDAY BRUNCH

Brunch is one of my favourite ways of entertaining. It doesn't matter whether it's indoors or out, it's a fine way to include the entire family.

It's all about jugs of fruit juices and glasses of bubbles with raspberries and strawberries, home bakes on lovely wooden boards, slices of fruit piled high on cake stands, tea and good-quality coffee. In our home, coffee is always a debatable matter – that's what happens when you marry an Italian! He likes latte macchiato. Me? I would settle for a simple, well-roasted Americano with a good dash of milk.

I like to make homemade jam when there's a glut of fresh fruits from the market and I delight in showing off my handiwork (don't we all need to give ourselves a good pat on the back from time to time?) by serving it with freshly baked warm scones and rustic loaves of bread. I try to prepare as much as possible the evening before – dough and batters can all be made the night before and kept in the fridge. My advice is to keep the warm dishes simple, like pancakes and French toast, and have fruit sliced and sauces prepared beforehand.

Platters are ideal for these occasions. Bring all the food to the table in one go and let everyone share and chat. Plus it's easier on you – no more running in and out of the kitchen. Just relax and enjoy the great company and delicious food.

3 FIGS, HALVED (OPTIONAL)

2 SMALL PEARS, HALVED AND THE CORE REMOVED WITH
A MELON BALLER, LEAVING THE STALKS ATTACHED

2 PLUMS, PITTED

2 NECTARINES, PITTED AND SLICED INTO WEDGES

125G BLACKBERRIES OR RASPBERRIES, WASHED

2 STAR ANISE

1 MEDIUM CINNAMON STICK

100G CASTER SUGAR

150ML WATER

60ML WHITE WINE

1 LEMON, ZESTED INTO STRIPS AND JUICED

CRÈME FRAÎCHE, TO SERVE

1 Preheat the oven to 180°C/fan 160°C/gas 4.

2 Place the prepared fruit into a large roasting tin. Add the star anise and cinnamon stick and sprinkle the sugar over evenly, then add the water and white wine. Stir in the lemon juice and zest. Carefully toss the fruit in the liquid.

3 Roast for 25–30 minutes, depending on the size of the fruit. It should be just softened and very slightly golden in colour. Serve warm or cold with a little crème fraîche.

A HEALTHY ONE
ROASTED FRUITS

Roasted fruit is elegant and delicious served with frozen yoghurt for a family occasion. Or layer slices of the juicy fruits with mascarpone and crushed biscotti in pretty glasses for a casual dinner party.

SERVES 4-6

A HEALTHY ONE
···············
BANANA AND APRICOT GRANOLA
···············

Begin the day with a good healthy start and spoon natural yoghurt over the granola. To treat your guests, why not make extra granola and package it in pretty bags with ribbons and a special note for each person as a farewell gift?

MAKES ABOUT 500G

350G PORRIDGE OATS

60G FLAKED ALMONDS

50G SUNFLOWER SEEDS

50G PUMPKIN SEEDS

4 TBSP SESAME SEEDS

3 TBSP COCONUT SHAVINGS

4 TBSP HONEY

2 TBSP RAPESEED OIL

12 READY-TO-EAT DRIED APRICOT HALVES, ROUGHLY CHOPPED

60G DRIED BANANA SLICES

1 Preheat the oven to 150°C/fan 130°C/gas 2. Line a large baking tray with parchment paper.

2 Mix the oats, almonds, seeds and coconut shavings in a large bowl and stir well. Drizzle in the honey and rapeseed oil and mix together. Pour out onto the lined tray and bake for about 20 minutes, stirring from time to time and keeping an eye on the granola, as it burns easily.

3 Remove from the oven and stir in the chopped apricots and banana slices. Cool completely before storing in a sealed jar. It will keep in a sealed container for up to 10 days.

A HEALTHY ONE

PASSION FRUIT, MANGO AND RASPBERRY YOGHURT LAYERS

This is a fun combination of cooked and fresh fruits. Make a compote from gooseberries when they are in season for drizzling over the top. Find all your different shaped glass-ware and spoon in layers of pretty fruit with the Greek yoghurt. It's so refreshing to sink a tall spoon down into the glasses to scoop out the wonderful fruity flavours.

SERVES 4

500G NATURAL GREEK YOGHURT
3 TBSP CLEAR HONEY
3 PASSION FRUITS
2 TBSP ICING SUGAR
1 MEDIUM MANGO, PEELED AND FINELY DICED

FOR THE RASPBERRY COMPOTE:
200G RASPBERRIES, WASHED
100G GOLDEN CASTER SUGAR
2 TBSP ELDERFLOWER CORDIAL OR 1TSP VANILLA EXTRACT

1 To make the raspberry compote, place the raspberries, sugar and cordial in a saucepan over a medium-low heat and simmer very gently for about 5 minutes, until the raspberries are just cooked. Set aside to cool.

2 Place the yoghurt in a medium bowl and mix in the honey to sweeten.

3 Slice the passion fruits in half and spoon the pulp out into a small bowl. Stir in the icing sugar.

4 Spoon the diced mango into 4 tall glasses. Add a yoghurt layer, spoon in some of the raspberry compote, then add another yoghurt layer. Carefully spoon the passion fruit pulp on the top layer. Place in the fridge to chill for about 20 minutes. If you keep this in the fridge longer than that, the raspberry compote will soak into the yoghurt, creating a pretty marbling effect.

250G LIGHT RYE FLOUR

120G ORGANIC WHOLE SPELT FLOUR

3 TBSP SUNFLOWER SEEDS, PLUS EXTRA TO DECORATE

1 TSP BREAD SODA

120ML NATURAL YOGHURT

100ML MILK

1 EGG, BEATEN

4 TBSP HONEY

2 TBSP RAPESEED OIL

1 TSP SALT

1 Preheat the oven to 200°C/fan 180°C/gas 6. Line a 900g loaf tin with parchment paper.

2 Combine the rye flour, spelt flour, sunflower seeds and bread soda in a large bowl.

3 Mix together the yoghurt, milk, egg, honey, rapeseed oil and salt in a separate bowl.

4 Pour most of the yoghurt mixture into the flour. Mix until a soft, sticky dough is formed, adding in more of the yoghurt if needed, then transfer to the loaf tin and sprinkle some sesame seeds on top. Bake for 25–30 minutes, until golden, well risen and cooked through. To know when bread is fully baked, tap the bottom of the bread – if it sounds hollow, then it's cooked. Or insert a skewer into the centre of the loaf – when it comes out clean, the bread is done. Cool on a wire rack before slicing.

A HEALTHY ONE
. . . .
RYE SODA BREAD
. . . .

I love having time to make my favourite homemade breads and rolls at the weekend. Making bread is much easier than you think. If you're making yeast bread, you just have to allow time for the rising process and there will be plenty of time to prepare other things in the meantime. Get creative with this recipe: try adding roughly chopped walnuts to make scones and bake them for 12–15 minutes.

MAKES 1 X 900G LOAF

A HEALTHY ONE

CHARGRILLED ASPARAGUS AND MUSHROOMS ON SOURDOUGH

This main course is very tasty. I might not have ordered this if I had seen it on a breakfast menu, but a friend who invited us to brunch many years ago, before brunch was a cool thing to do, served this and it has become one of my favourites.

SERVES 4

12 THIN ASPARAGUS SPEARS, TRIMMED
EXTRA VIRGIN OLIVE OIL
30G BUTTER
100G MUSHROOMS, STALKS REMOVED AND SLICED
2 TSP CHOPPED FRESH TARRAGON
SALT AND FRESHLY GROUND BLACK PEPPER
4 SLICES SOURDOUGH BREAD, TOASTED

1 Preheat a chargrill pan over a medium heat. Brush the asparagus spears with extra virgin olive oil and cook for 2–3 minutes on both sides, until tender.

2 In the meantime, heat a large frying pan over a medium heat and melt the butter. Add the sliced mushrooms and tarragon and sauté for 3–4 minutes, until just cooked. Season with salt and freshly ground black pepper.

3 Brush the sourdough with a little extra virgin olive oil and toast in the chargrill pan.

4 To serve, place the toasted sourdough on a plate. Pile the tarragon mushrooms on the toast and arrange 3 asparagus spears on top. Serve immediately.

1 TSP WHITE WINE VINEGAR

4 EGGS

4 THIN SLICES BLACK PUDDING, COOKED

4 SLICES SODA BREAD, TOASTED

FOR THE HOLLANDAISE SAUCE:

2 EGG YOLKS

125G BUTTER, DICED

1 TSP LEMON JUICE

1 To make the hollandaise sauce, place the egg yolks in a bowl set over a saucepan of gently simmering water (bain marie) and whisk thoroughly.

2 Add the butter one piece at a time, whisking constantly. As soon as one piece melts, add the next piece. The mixture will gradually thicken, but if it shows signs of becoming too thick or even scrambling, remove the pan from the heat immediately and plunge the base of the saucepan into a bowl of iced water. Do not leave the pan or stop whisking until the sauce is made.

3 Stir in the lemon juice to taste. If the sauce doesn't thicken quickly, it might be because you are being a little too careful and that the heat is too low. Increase the heat just slightly and continue to whisk until the sauce thickens to a coating consistency. If the sauce is too thick, add 1 tablespoon of cold water. Keep the sauce warm over a bowl of warm water. Hollandaise sauce should not be reheated.

4 To poach the eggs, fill a medium saucepan with water and bring to the boil. Add the vinegar and reduce the heat to a gentle simmer, then stir the water to form a vortex. Carefully break in the egg and poach for 2 $\frac{1}{2}$-3 minutes, depending on how you like your egg.

5 Once the egg is cooked, lift it out of the water with a slotted spoon and drain the water off. Arrange a slice of black pudding on the toasted soda bread and place the egg on top. Spoon a little hollandaise sauce over and serve immediately.

THE IRISH ONE

EGGS BENEDICT, IRISH STYLE

When making hollandaise sauce, it's important not to let your saucepan get too hot. You should be able to place your hand comfortably on the side of the saucepan at any stage. Keep a bowl of iced water nearby so that you can plunge the base of the saucepan into it if it gets too hot. Keep this classic sauce recipe to hand so that you can whip it up in a flash to spoon over other dishes, like steak.

SERVES 4

THE IRISH ONE

ALL-IN-ONE IRISH BREAKFAST BAKE

If you aren't making this for brunch, it also works really well for match food or late night suppers and it's much easier than making the usual fry-up. Choose good-quality sausages from your local butcher. It's the easy way out, a one-pot breakfast that saves on the washing up, a definite crowd pleaser and it's delicious – can it get any better?

SERVES 4

RAPESEED OIL
2 MEDIUM POTATOES, SLICED INTO WEDGES
8 GOOD-QUALITY BREAKFAST SAUSAGES
10–12 CHERRY TOMATOES
8 LARGE MUSHROOMS, WIPED CLEAN
SALT AND FRESHLY GROUND BLACK PEPPER
4 EGGS
CHOPPED FRESH PARSLEY, TO GARNISH
TOAST, TO SERVE

1 Preheat the oven to 180°C/fan 160°C/gas 4. Brush an ovenproof, shallow casserole or roasting skillet with oil.

2 Place the potato wedges into the casserole dish or skillet and roast in the oven for about 12 minutes.

3 Add the sausages and cook for a further 10 minutes, turning them over once or twice during the cooking time.

4 Add the cherry tomatoes and mushrooms to the casserole dish or skillet. Drizzle a little more oil over the vegetables and season. Cook until the potato wedges are crispy and the tomatoes are roasted.

5 Make 4 gaps in between the vegetables and carefully break an egg into each. Season lightly with salt and freshly ground black pepper. Return to the oven and cook for a further 5–6 minutes, until the eggs are set. Sprinkle with chopped fresh parsley and serve immediately with toast.

6 SHEETS FILO PASTRY

50G BUTTER, MELTED

200G SMALL CHERRY TOMATOES, SOME WHOLE AND
  OTHERS HALVED

1 TBSP EXTRA VIRGIN OLIVE OIL

1 TBSP BALSAMIC VINEGAR

4 SPRIGS FRESH THYME, PLUS EXTRA TO GARNISH

100G MOZZARELLA, TORN INTO SMALL PIECES

7 FRESH BASIL LEAVES, PLUS EXTRA TO GARNISH

2 TBSP SHOP-BOUGHT BASIL PESTO

SALT AND FRESHLY GROUND BLACK PEPPER

THE ITALIANO
CAPRESE TARTLETS

Using filo pastry is very convenient, especially when you have a large crowd coming over. I like to keep a close eye on the filo when these tartlets are baking, as they have sometimes come out of the oven a little darker than I wanted them. Cutting filo can be a bit difficult sometimes, so I use a clean pair of scissors. Why don't you try a fruit version of this, with melon balls, black grapes and blackberries, with mint leaves and a cassis mascarpone spooned over the fruit?

1 Preheat the oven to 180°C/fan 160°C/gas 4. Brush a 12-hole muffin tin with melted butter, making sure to brush the top of the tin as well.

2 Place a sheet of filo pastry on a board and brush with melted butter. Add 2 more sheets on top, brushing each with butter. Cut in half lengthways and then cut into 6 rectangles. Repeat the process with the other 3 sheets of filo. Line the muffin tin with the filo pieces and brush a little melted butter over each pastry case.

3 Bake for 6–7 minutes, until golden brown and crisp. Keep an eye on the filo to make sure it doesn't get too dark.

4 Meanwhile, to make the filling, line a baking tray with parchment paper. Place the cherry tomatoes on the tray, drizzle over the extra virgin olive oil and balsamic vinegar and scatter over the sprigs of thyme. Roast for 15–18 minutes, then transfer to a bowl and set aside to cool.

5 Add the mozzarella to the roasted tomatoes together with the basil leaves. Spoon in the pesto and check the seasoning.

6 Carefully remove the pastry cases from the muffin tray and spoon the filling into the crispy filo pastry. Garnish each tartlet with a sprig of thyme or basil leaves and serve immediately.

MAKES 12

THE ITALIANO
CHOCOLATE BRIOCHE AND CARAMEL ICE CREAM SANDWICH

This reminds me of the brioche buns filled with gorgeous ice cream in Sicily. If it's raining you might have the time to make your own ice cream, but why would you be making ice cream if there's no sunshine? The chocolate and cardamom buns on page 85 would be ideal for this sandwich.

SERVES 4

8 SMALL SLICES BRIOCHE
4 TBSP CHOCOLATE HAZELNUT SPREAD
300G CARAMEL ICE CREAM BLOCK

1 Toast the slices of brioche, and if they are too large, stamp out circles with a large scone cutter. Thinly coat one side of each piece of toast with some of the chocolate hazelnut spread.

2 Using a hot knife, slice the ice cream to fit the size of the brioche toast and sandwich the ice cream in between the bread. Serve immediately.

FOR THE PANCAKES:
220G PLAIN FLOUR
1 TSP BAKING POWDER
½ TSP BREAD SODA
1 TBSP CASTER SUGAR
½ TSP SALT
2 LARGE EGGS, BEATEN
300ML MILK
SUNFLOWER OIL

FOR THE MARSALA SYRUP:
60G CASTER SUGAR
100ML WATER
80ML MARSALA (OR ORANGE JUICE, IF SERVING TO KIDS)

FOR THE FRUIT:
1 SMALL PINEAPPLE, PEELED AND VERY THINLY SLICED
16 SEEDLESS RED GRAPES, WASHED AND DESTALKED
100G BLUEBERRIES, WASHED

1 To make the syrup, place the sugar, water and Marsala into a small saucepan and bring to the boil. Reduce the heat and simmer for about 15 minutes, until the sugar has dissolved and a thick syrup forms. Set aside to cool completely.

2 To make the pancakes, sieve the flour, baking powder and bread soda into a large bowl. Stir in the sugar and salt. Make a well in the centre and add the beaten egg and enough milk to form a stiff batter. Allow the batter to rest for 20 minutes. If you feel the batter is too stiff at this stage, add 2 tablespoons of milk and stir to combine.

3 Heat some oil in a large frying pan over a medium heat. Using a ladle, spoon in the batter around the pan, making circular shapes, and cook for 1–2 minutes, until small bubbles appear on the top. Turn the pancakes over and cook for a further 1–2 minutes, until they are golden brown. Keep the pancakes warm.

4 To assemble for brunch, pile up all the warm pancakes on a large warm platter. Add layers of pineapple, sprinkle over the red grapes and blueberries and pour over some of the Marsala syrup.

THE ALL-AMERICAN ONE

PANCAKES WITH FRESH FRUITS AND MARSALA SYRUP

I like to see stacks of pancakes piled up on plates. If you prefer, you could pour a good-quality warmed maple syrup over the top of them instead of the Marsala syrup. The colourful fresh fruit not only looks pretty, but adds a healthy angle to this recipe. I have also served a sweet basil drizzle, which is really brilliant with the pineapple.

MAKES 12

THE ALL-AMERICAN ONE

CHOCOLATE FRENCH TOAST WITH HAZELNUTS, RASPBERRIES AND MAPLE SYRUP

There is only a hint of choco-late in this one and the rasp-berries balance out the sweet-ness well. Or at least that's my theory! You can slice brioche buns lengthways or even use slices of barm brack for a deli-cious French toast.

SERVES 4

3 EGGS, BEATEN
100ML MILK
3 TBSP COCOA POWDER, SIEVED
3 TBSP ICING SUGAR, SIEVED, PLUS EXTRA FOR DUSTING
¼ TSP GROUND CINNAMON
SUNFLOWER OIL
4 SLICES BRIOCHE, EACH SLICE CUT IN HALF
100G RASPBERRIES, WASHED
3 TBSP HAZELNUTS, TOASTED AND ROUGHLY CHOPPED
MAPLE SYRUP, TO SERVE

1 Whisk together the eggs, milk, cocoa powder, icing sugar and cinnamon in a large, shallow bowl.

2 Heat a little oil in a large non-stick frying pan over a medium heat. Using a fork, dip both sides of the bread into the chocolate egg batter and place into the frying pan. Cook until lightly golden on both sides. Transfer to a serving plate and dust with the icing sugar. Sprinkle over some raspberries and hazelnuts and drizzle over the maple syrup. Serve immediately.

FOR THE MUFFINS:

3 EGGS

225G GOLDEN CASTER
SUGAR

120ML RAPESEED OIL

100ML MILK

1 TSP VANILLA

300G SELF-RAISING FLOUR

½ TSP BAKING POWDER

ZEST OF ½ ORANGE

100G BLUEBERRIES,
WASHED

3 TBSP WALNUTS, ROUGHLY
CHOPPED

FOR THE TOPPING:

120G BUTTER, SOFTENED

350G ICING SUGAR

80G CRÈME FRAÎCHE

ZEST AND JUICE OF ½
ORANGE

12 WALNUTS, TO DECORATE

A FEW BLUEBERRIES, TO
DECORATE

*FOR THE CINNAMON COFFEE
(SERVES 1):*

A LARGE SERVING OF GOOD
COFFEE

2 TSP CASTER SUGAR, OR
TO TASTE

½ TSP GROUND CINNAMON

60ML LOW-FAT MILK

CINNAMON STICK, TO
GARNISH

1 Preheat the oven to 180°C/fan 160°C/ gas 4. Line a 12-hole muffin tray with muffin cases.

2 Whisk the eggs, sugar, oil, milk and vanilla together until thick and pale. Carefully fold in the flour and baking powder, then mix in the orange zest. Stir in the blueberries and walnuts and spoon the mixture into the muffin cases (a ladle works very well for this).

3 Bake for 20-25 minutes, until golden and a skewer inserted into the centre comes out clean. Cool completely before piping on the topping.

4 To make the topping, cream the butter until pale and fluffy. Slowly add the icing sugar and keep beating. Add the crème fraîche and fold in the orange zest and juice.

5 Spoon the topping into a piping bag and decorate the muffins. Place walnuts or blueberries on top of each muffin.

6 Pour the coffee into a serving mug, then stir in the sugar and cinnamon. Froth the milk with a whisk or frother and carefully spoon it on top of the cinnamon coffee. Garnish with a cinnamon stick and serve immediately with the muffins.

THE ALL-AMERICAN ONE
BLUEBERRY AND WALNUT MUFFINS WITH CINNAMON COFFEE

The rapeseed oil gives these muffins a pale yellow hue, which is a pretty contrast with the blueberries. Use smaller cupcake cases for daintier versions.

MAKES 12 MUFFINS

1 EGG

100G PLAIN FLOUR

20G SPINACH, WASHED AND VERY FINELY SHREDDED

160ML MILK

2 TBSP MELTED BUTTER, PLUS EXTRA FOR COOKING

2 TSP CHOPPED FRESH CHIVES

½ TSP BAKING POWDER

SALT AND FRESHLY GROUND BLACK PEPPER

WATERCRESS, TO GARNISH

FOR THE FILLING:

30G BUTTER

ZEST AND JUICE OF 1 LEMON

2 TSP CHOPPED FRESH CHIVES

6 THIN SLICES SMOKED SALMON, CUT INTO STRIPS

A GOOD HANDFUL OF BABY SPINACH, WASHED AND
  TRIMMED

SCANDI STYLE
SALMON WITH SPINACH AND CHIVE CRÊPES

The dry ingredients can be mixed together the night before so that all you have to do is add the liquid and spinach in the morning. Keep layering the crêpes in between sheets of parchment paper so they don't stick together.

MAKES 6 MEDIUM CRÊPES

1 To make the crêpes, whisk together the egg, flour, spinach, milk, melted butter, chives and salt and pepper in a jug until smooth. Allow to stand for about 1 hour.

2 To make the filling, melt the butter in a saucepan over a medium heat. Add the lemon zest and juice and the chives and mix well. Add the smoked salmon and spinach and cook for 1–2 minutes, until the spinach is wilted. Set aside and keep warm.

3 To cook the crêpes, heat a large non-stick pan with a little butter over a medium heat. When the pan is hot, pour in a little batter, swirling the pan to evenly coat the base with batter. Cook for a few minutes, until golden, and flip over and cook the other side. Place on a warm plate, cover with a sheet of parchment paper and continue to make more crêpes with the rest of the batter. Keep warm.

4 To assemble, fold a crêpe into quarters on a serving plate and spoon in the filling. Arrange a little watercress to the side and serve.

MELON, MANGO AND LEMONGRASS SMOOTHIE

This is sunshine in a glass. You could try it without the melon and add strawberries instead, but I don't think I would change it at all. It's lovely after a long hike into the countryside, as the lemongrass is very energising.

SERVES 4

2 MANGOS, PEELED AND ROUGHLY DICED
1 CANTALOUPE MELON, PEELED AND DICED
1 LEMONGRASS STALK, ROUGHLY CHOPPED
1 TBSP HONEY (OPTIONAL)
ICE, TO SERVE

1 Place the mangos, melon and lemongrass in a blender or smoothie maker and process until smooth. Check for sweetness and add the honey to taste. Pour into tall glasses with ice.

STRAWBERRY AND PEACH BREAKFAST FIZZ

....

100G STRAWBERRIES, WASHED AND HULLED, PLUS
  6 TO GARNISH
2 PEACHES, PEELED, STONE REMOVED AND DICED
2 TBSP ICING SUGAR
1 BOTTLE SPARKLING WINE

1 Place the strawberries and diced peaches into a food processor or blender and process until very smooth. Pour the purée through a sieve into a jug, then add the icing sugar and stir well, until the sugar dissolves.

2 Pour about 50ml of the fruit purée into chilled champagne flutes and carefully top with the sparkling wine. Just be careful not to fill the champagne flutes too fast, or they will bubble over and make a mess.

3 Using a sharp knife, cut a small incision in the bottom of each strawberry so that it can be attached to the rim of the glass. Serve immediately.

When making fruit purées, if you need extra sweetness, add icing sugar instead of caster sugar, as it dissolves easily in the thick fruit purée. You can also make fruit ice cubes by pouring a little purée into your favourite ice cube shape, then add a sprig of rosemary or a raspberry into each cube and freeze.

SERVES 6

SUNDAY LUNCH

'ALL THAT MEAT AND NO POTATOES' - FATS WALLER

'SING FOR YOUR SUPPER' - THE MAMAS AND THE PAPAS

'LET'S CALL THE WHOLE THING OFF' - THE GERSHWINS

CHAPTER 11 } SUNDAY LUNCH

The perfect Sunday for me is a big gang of family and friends around the table on a lazy afternoon. Sunday lunch is an institution here at Ballyknocken House. For me, it's also a nostalgic experience, remembering the fun we had as kids over lunch on Sundays. I love recreating this with my family – we even get the deck of cards out to play Pontoon! Homemade and delicious are my key thoughts on Sunday lunch, but I also like it to be easy and relaxed.

Sunday lunch doesn't have to break the budget either. A chicken or pork belly is ideally priced, but if it's a special Sunday lunch, then a rib of beef on the bone or a beef fillet with a rub or encrusted herbs would be a superb treat.

Here's a guide to choosing cuts of meat for your Sunday lunch thanks to our local butcher, Robert Cullen.

ROAST FILLET	Very tender, but will dry out and can be overcooked. Perfect for beef Wellington.
SIRLOIN ROAST	Great flavour and tenderness. Can be cooked on or off the bone.
PRIME RIB ROAST	Best all-round depth of flavour and tenderness. Good value.
TOP RIB ROAST	Ideal for pot roast (slow roast with liquid).
EYE OF ROUND	Very lean. Needs to be kept covered (add some liquid).
ROUND ROAST	Great value, but not as tender as rib roast. Ideal for slow cooking.
BRISKET	Ideal for pot roast, as seen in US & UK cookbooks. Needs to be cooked very slowly.
BEEF SHORT RIBS	Slowly braised in wine or beer with vegetables and loads of aromatics, these will have fantastic flavour.

GREEK LAMB WITH FETA TOPPING

....

I wouldn't say that this is your usual roast leg of lamb, but I do love a little Greek influence and the wonderful, classic flavours of lemon and oregano. Lamb is always a winner and you can't go wrong with a casserole, which gives you time to get ready for the week ahead or just spend with your family.

SERVES 4-6

EXTRA VIRGIN OLIVE OIL
1KG LAMB SHOULDER, DICED INTO 3CM PIECES
5 SHALLOTS, SLICED
2 CARROTS, PEELED AND FINELY DICED
1 X 400G TIN CHOPPED TOMATOES
800ML VEGETABLE STOCK
2 BAY LEAVES
1 CINNAMON STICK
ZEST OF ½ LEMON
1 TBSP TOMATO PURÉE
2 TSP CHOPPED FRESH OREGANO
¼ TSP GROUND CINNAMON
SALT AND FRESHLY GROUND BLACK PEPPER
120G PEARL BARLEY
6 BLACK OLIVES, TO GARNISH
1 TBSP CHOPPED FRESH PARSLEY
FETA CHEESE, CRUMBLED, TO GARNISH
6 LEMON SLICES OR WEDGES, TO GARNISH

1 Preheat the oven to 180°C/fan 160°C/gas 4.

2 Heat a large frying pan with extra virgin olive oil over a medium heat and sear the lamb all over, then place in a casserole dish. Sauté the shallots in the frying pan for about 5 minutes, then transfer to the casserole. Add the carrots, tomatoes, stock, bay leaves, cinnamon stick, lemon zest, tomato purée, oregano, ground cinnamon and some salt and pepper to the casserole, then cover with a lid.

3 Increase the heat and bring to the boil, then place in the oven for 1½ hours, stirring from time to time. Remove the bay leaves and cinnamon stick and stir in the barley. Cook for a further 30-40 minutes, until the barley thickens the sauce and is soft. Spoon off any excess fat that has risen to the top.

4 Allow to rest for about 10 minutes. To serve, stir through the olives and parsley, crumble the feta cheese over the top and arrange a few slices or wedges of lemon on top.

o" di Monti

: l'Italia non è Cipro

possibilità che esistono con il contributo del nuovo Parlamento». Fino a quando non si sa. Ma mette subito in rampa di lancio i decreti sul pagamento dei debiti della Pubblica amministrazione che per il premier «potrebbero essere pronti nei prossimi giorni». E si mette a lavorare di lena sul Piano nazionale delle riforme e sul Documento di economia e finanza da consegnare a Bruxelles entro fine aprile. Lo stesso Monti potrebbe andare nella capitale belga a illustrare informalmente le loro linee guida, cogliendo l'occasione per rassicurare l'Europa sull'o... ... mità del governo (non per niente ... ... sione che lavora alla «preparazio... ... che un messaggio all'opportu...

... rità che qualche ministro vada a Berli-no, Londra e Washington per spiegare alle Cancellerie e ai big della finanza che «l'Italia non è alla deriva».

Altre iniziative, spiegano da Palazzo Chigi, il governo le potrebbe prendere su impulso del Parlamento o d... ste... e commissioni di saggi: «Conf... eremo la nostra ...enda con loro», garantiscono dal governo. Intanto l'Europa cerca di dare una mano: il portavoce della Commissione esprime «fi...ucia nel processo democratico italiano» per trovare la giusta soluzione» e il ministro delle Finanze tedesco, Wolfgang Schaeuble, rassicura che «non c'è pericolo che l'Italia sia una nuova Cipro».

1.2KG BONELESS PORK BELLY, SKIN SCORED

2 TSP SALT

EXTRA VIRGIN OLIVE OIL

4 TBSP DARK BROWN SUGAR

JUICE OF 1 LEMON

FOR THE FENNEL AND CHILLI RUB:

2 TSP FENNEL SEEDS

2 GARLIC CLOVES

1 TSP SEA SALT

1 RED CHILLI, FINELY CHOPPED

1 X 2CM PIECE OF FRESH GINGER, PEELED AND GRATED

2 TBSP DARK BROWN SUGAR

2 TBSP EXTRA VIRGIN OLIVE OIL

FOR THE SWEET POTATOES:

EXTRA VIRGIN OLIVE OIL

2 LARGE SWEET POTATOES, PEELED AND DICED INTO 2CM PIECES

1 X 2CM PIECE OF FRESH GINGER, PEELED AND SLICED INTO FINE JULIENNE

SALT AND FRESHLY GROUND BLACK PEPPER

CRISPY PORK BELLY WITH CHILLI GINGER CARAMEL AND SWEET POTATOES

....

Start cooking the pork early – not only will this have those wonderful aromas escaping from the kitchen, but the pork will be soft and juicy and the crackling will be crispy and tasty, and your family will love you for that. Instead of serving this with an apple compote or sauce, I have often served it with roasted plums, which blend very well with the fennel seeds and the ginger. It would also be delicious sliced into thick strips and served while watching the match with a bottle of craft beer.

SERVES 4

1 To make the rub, toast the fennel seeds in a dry frying pan over a medium heat for about 30 seconds. Grind the fennel seeds in a pestle and mortar with the garlic and sea salt. Transfer to a small bowl and add the chilli, ginger, brown sugar and oil. Retain 2 teaspoons to sprinkle over the pork at the end of the cooking time. Rub the rest over the skin of the pork belly and allow the flavours to develop for a few hours or even overnight.

2 Preheat the oven to 200°C/fan 180°C/gas 6.

3 Place the pork belly in a roasting tin and rub the skin with the salt and some oil. Roast the meat for 20 minutes, then reduce the heat to 180°C/fan 160°C/gas 4. Mix the brown sugar and lemon juice together and drizzle over the pork. Return the meat to the oven and roast for a further 1 hour 30 minutes, basting from time to time.

4 About half an hour before the end of the pork belly's cooking time, drizzle a large roasting tin with a little extra virgin olive oil and heat for 2 minutes in the oven. Add the sweet potatoes and the ginger julienne and toss well, then season with salt and freshly ground black pepper. Roast for 20-25 minutes, turning from time to time. Once cooked, remove from the oven and keep warm.

5 Increase the heat to 220°C/fan 200°C/gas 7 and roast the pork for a final 15 minutes to finish the crackling, keeping an eye on it to make sure it doesn't burn. Sprinkle over the reserved 2 teaspoons of the chilli and ginger rub and allow to rest for 10 minutes loosely covered with foil. Carve into thick slices and serve with the ginger sweet potatoes.

4 CHICKEN SUPREMES, TRIMMED
100G SPINACH, WASHED AND TRIMMED
RAPESEED OIL
100G FETA CHEESE, CRUMBLED
SALT AND FRESHLY GROUND BLACK PEPPER
4 LONG FRESH ROSEMARY SPRIGS

FOR THE TOPPING:
ZEST OF 1 ORANGE
60G PANKO OR BREADCRUMBS
2 TBSP RAPESEED OIL
1 TBSP CHOPPED FRESH PARSLEY
1 TSP CHOPPED FRESH OREGANO
½–1 TSP PAPRIKA, TO TASTE
SALT AND FRESHLY GROUND BLACK PEPPER

1 Preheat the oven to 180°C/fan 160°C/gas 4.

2 Make an incision along the side of each supreme to make a 'pocket' to stuff with the filling.

3 Place the spinach in a medium saucepan over a medium-low heat with a little rapeseed oil and wilt. Allow to cool.

4 Mix together the cooled spinach and feta cheese in a bowl and season with salt and freshly ground black pepper. Spoon the spinach and feta into the pocket of the supreme, taking care not to overfill it. If needed, you can secure the pocket by threading a rosemary sprig through the chicken.

5 Mix together all the topping ingredients in a bowl and season with salt and freshly ground black pepper.

6 Place the chicken supremes in a roasting tin drizzled with a little rapeseed oil and roast for 20 minutes. Take the supremes out of the oven and spoon the breadcrumb topping over each one. Drizzle with a little more rapeseed oil and return to the oven for a further 15 minutes, or until the supremes are fully cooked.

7 Arrange on a serving platter and drizzle over the pan juices. Serve immediately.

CHICKEN SUPREMES WITH PAPRIKA ORANGE CRUNCH TOPPING

....

Double or triple this recipe and serve these chicken supremes on a large, pretty platter for family gatherings and special occasions. This chicken is also delicious with salads for the warmer summer months or with a large homely gratin and roasted potatoes when it's cooler.

SERVES 4

THE PERFECT SUNDAY ROAST

··

Chicken comes to mind when I think of Sunday roast, but my favourite is thin slices of roast beef, sweet and caramelised on the outside, pink on the inside. Some of us worry about preparing the Sunday roast for family and friends, but in my opinion it's all down to good-quality produce and timing. Purchase the best free-range chicken that you can afford as well as good-quality beef from a butcher that supports local farmers.

Here's a countdown. This example is for preparing roast chicken, roast beef, roast potatoes, thyme and honey carrots and, of course, the wonderful gravy.

ROAST CHICKEN

Cooking time
1 hour 30 minutes, depending on size. Allow 15 minutes per 500g plus an additional 15 minutes. If stuffing the chicken, weigh it after stuffing it and then calculate the cooking time.

Preheated oven temperature
First 15 minutes: 220°C/fan 200°C/gas mark 7, then reduce to 190°C/fan 170°C/gas mark 5.

1 Mix a blend of your favourite flavourings or spices as a rub to infuse flavour into the chicken, e.g. lemon zest, dried oregano, salt and pepper; or cumin, orange zest, salt and pepper. Allow the rub to infuse for at least 2 hours and take the chicken out of the fridge about 15 minutes before roasting.

2 Place the chicken on a bed of root vegetables (such as carrots, parsnips and onions) with a drizzle of extra virgin olive oil, some sprigs of fresh thyme and a few cloves of garlic. Baste the chicken about every 15 minutes or wrap pancetta over the chicken breasts to prevent them from drying out.

ROAST SIRLOIN OF BEEF

Cooking time
Generally, 15 minutes per 500g plus an additional 15 minutes for medium. Allow 12 minutes per 500g for rare or 20 minutes per 500g for well done.

Preheated oven temperature
First 15 minutes: 220°C/fan 200°C/gas mark 7, then reduce to 190°C/fan 170°C/gas mark 5.

1 Season the beef with salt and freshly ground black pepper and perhaps a little chopped fresh thyme and rosemary, or try an Italian twist of olive oil, some dried oregano, powdered garlic, salt and pepper.

2 The key to cooking roast beef is to let it rest for 15 minutes before serving. During this time, you can make the gravy by skimming the fat from the roasting tray and then deglazing with a little stock, wine or water to loosen all those wonderful caramelised juices, and finally thickening with a little roux and seasoning to taste.

ROAST POTATOES

Preparation time
20 minutes

Cooking time
35–45 minutes, depending on size

1 I think Roosters and Golden Wonders are probably the most popular potatoes and roast the best. You want a crispy outside and a soft yet dry interior. For a difference, try roast sweet potato wedges with a sprinkling of brown sugar, cumin and harissa.

THYME AND HONEY CARROTS

Preparation time
15 minutes

Cooking time
25 minutes

1 Thyme and honey is a perfect match and is what you want for Sunday lunch. Slice the carrots diagonally, steam them and then toss in a saucepan with chopped fresh thyme and honey or maple syrup.

GRAVY

Preparation time
3–4 minutes

Cooking time
10 minutes

1 Gravy is as important as the potatoes. When your chicken or beef is resting, begin by draining off the fat from the roasting tin. Place the tin on the hob and stir in 2 or 3 tablespoons of plain flour or 3 tablespoons of mashed potato. Stir to form a smooth paste, then keep stirring to cook. Add chicken or beef stock, stirring all the time. Mind that lumps don't form and be sure to scrape up all the 'bits' from the bottom of the tin. Cook for 2–3 minutes and season to taste.

2KG BEEF RIB, ON THE BONE
SALT AND FRESHLY GROUND BLACK PEPPER
EXTRA VIRGIN OLIVE OIL
6 SHALLOTS, HALVED
4 CARROTS, ROUGHLY CHOPPED
4 LARGE SPRIGS OF FRESH THYME
2 WHOLE GARLIC BULBS, SLICED IN HALF

FOR THE GRAVY:
1 BOTTLE RED WINE
400ML BEEF STOCK

1 Preheat the oven to 220°C/fan 200°C/gas 7.

2 Season the beef with salt and freshly ground black pepper.

3 Heat some extra virgin olive oil in a large frying pan over a high heat and sear the meat on all sides, including the ends, until golden brown. Set aside.

4 Make a bed of shallots, carrots, thyme and garlic in a large roasting tin. Drizzle with a little extra virgin olive oil and sit the beef on top of the vegetables. Roast for 20 minutes, then reduce the heat to 160°C/fan 140°C/gas 3 and continue to cook for 20 minutes per 500g for medium or 15 minutes per 500g for rare. Transfer the beef to a plate, cover with foil to keep warm and allow to rest for 25 minutes.

5 To make the gravy, place the roasting tin over a medium heat. Pour the red wine into the tin, scraping up all the caramelised bits on the bottom of the tin. Bring to the boil, then reduce to a simmer and cook until the wine has reduced by half. Pour in the stock and the juices caught on the plate beneath the beef. Pass the gravy through a sieve to remove the vegetables.

6 Transfer the beef to a serving platter ready for carving and pour the gravy into a jug. Leftover gravy can be frozen and served later with bangers and mash for a tasty supper.

ROAST RIB OF BEEF
· · · · · · · · · ·

This is such an amazing piece of meat that I wouldn't do much to it at all – it speaks for itself. Choose Quality Assured beef, which should be a dark red colour with a marbling of fat.

SERVES 6

WHOLE SEABREAM WITH CHILLI AND LIME MOJO

MELTED BUTTER, FOR GREASING

1KG NEW POTATOES, SKIN ON AND DICED INTO
  2CM PIECES

8 SPRING ONIONS, SLICED LENGTHWAYS

2 RED PEPPERS, SLICED

SUNFLOWER OIL

SALT AND FRESHLY GROUND BLACK PEPPER

2 X 1.2KG WHOLE SEABREAM, SCALED AND GUTTED

2 LIMES (ZEST OF 2 AND JUICE OF 1)

1 RED CHILLI, FINELY CHOPPED

2 TBSP CHOPPED FRESH DILL

2 TSP MAPLE SYRUP

1 TSP HARISSA

FRESH DILL SPRIGS, TO GARNISH

LIME WEDGES, TO GARNISH

1 Preheat the oven to 180°C/fan 160°C/gas 4.

2 Place the potatoes, spring onions and red peppers in a roasting tin and drizzle with sunflower oil, then season with salt and freshly ground black pepper.

3 Place the 2 whole seabream on top of the vegetables and drizzle with a little more sunflower oil.

4 Mix the lime zest and juice, chilli, dill, maple syrup and harissa together and spoon over the fish. Cook for about 20 minutes. Check that the fish is done by carefully inserting a sharp knife and pulling away the flesh to ensure the fish flakes easily. Garnish with dill sprigs and lime wedges and serve immediately.

Is there such a thing as a party platter that's also healthy? This easygoing combination of ingredients gives the seabream a delicate sour and sweet flavour, but it's not overpowering. Serve with purple sprouting broccoli and a spinach and chickpea salad with a lime dressing. It's one of those recipes that makes me feel happy when preparing it, though I can't pinpoint what it is – perhaps the blend of lime, maple syrup and spice?

SERVES 6-8

1 X 4KG OVEN-READY GOOSE
2 TSP FIVE SPICE POWDER
SALT AND FRESHLY GROUND BLACK PEPPER

FOR THE PEARS:
100G LIGHT BROWN SUGAR
700ML RED WINE (MERLOT IS A GOOD CHOICE)
200ML WATER
2 STAR ANISE
1 CINNAMON STICK
1 BAY LEAF, PLUS EXTRA TO GARNISH
5 MEDIUM PEARS, PEELED AND CORED WITH THE
   STALKS LEFT ON

GOOSE WITH RED WINE SYRUP AND PEARS

The general rule of thumb for roasting goose is to cook it for 10 minutes at 240°C/fan 220°C/gas 9, then reduce the heat to 190°C/fan 170°C/gas 7 and roast for 30 minutes per kg, plus the resting time of 25 minutes.

SERVES 6-8

1 Weigh the goose and check the inside of the bird for giblets and remove the fat pads. Rub the five spice powder over the goose, then prick the breast and legs with a fork and set aside, covered, for 30 minutes.

2 Meanwhile, add the sugar, wine, water, star anise, cinnamon and bay leaf to a large saucepan over a medium-high heat and bring to the boil. Reduce the heat and simmer for 10-12 minutes, until a syrup forms. Reduce the heat to low and add the pears to the syrup. Simmer for 5-6 minutes, until just softened. Remove from the heat and set aside.

3 To cook the goose, preheat the oven to 240°C/fan 220°C/gas 9. Transfer the goose to a large roasting tin and season with salt and pepper. Roast the goose for the calculated time (see the intro), reducing the heat to 190°C/fan 170°C/gas 5 after the first 10 minutes. If the bird is browning too quickly, slide a piece of foil over the top. Baste the bird every 20 minutes with the pan juices and some red wine syrup from the poached pears. At the end of the roasting time, transfer the goose to a serving platter. Arrange the pears and bay leaves around the goose and spoon over a little pear syrup. Cover with foil and leave in a warm area to rest for 20 minutes before carving.

MELTED BUTTER, FOR GREASING

EXTRA VIRGIN OLIVE OIL

2 LARGE LEEKS, THINLY SLICED

2 GARLIC CLOVES, CHOPPED

900G SWEET POTATOES (ABOUT 3 MEDIUM POTATOES),
   PEELED AND THINLY SLICED

SALT AND FRESHLY GROUND BLACK PEPPER

70G FRESHLY GRATED PARMESAN

FRESHLY GRATED NUTMEG

300ML DOUBLE CREAM

1 Preheat the oven to 180°C/fan 160°C/gas 4. Brush a square 20cm ovenproof dish with melted butter.

2 Heat a large frying pan with extra virgin olive oil over a medium heat and sauté the leeks for about 6 minutes, until just softened. Add the garlic and cook for 2 minutes more.

3 Arrange a layer of sweet potato slices on the bottom of the dish. Season with a little salt and some freshly ground black pepper and layer with the sautéed leeks and garlic, sprinkling over some of the Parmesan in between. Repeat this process of layering, ending with the cheese on top.

4 Grate a little nutmeg into the cream and pour it over the potatoes and leeks. Cook in the oven for about 40 minutes, pressing the potatoes down into the cream from time to time, until the potatoes are soft and the top is crisp and golden brown. Allow the gratin to cool slightly before serving.

SWEET POTATO AND LEEK GRATIN

....

Make this in smaller gratin dishes to serve individually at a dinner party. Prepare them ahead of time and heat when ready. If you're counting the calories, use half homemade vegetable stock and half cream.

SERVES 4-6

FENNEL, CHARD AND ASPARAGUS LIME STIR-FRY

....

This is a fantastic side dish that's also great served with rice for a late night supper. The vegetables can be swapped out with whatever you already have in the kitchen or garden.

SERVES 4

2 TBSP SUNFLOWER OIL
1 ONION, FINELY SLICED
1 MEDIUM FENNEL BULB, FINELY SLICED
2 TSP SOY SAUCE
1 TSP OYSTER SAUCE
1 TSP HONEY
½ TSP HOT CHILLI SAUCE
JUICE AND ZEST OF 1 LIME
10 THIN ASPARAGUS SPEARS, SLICED LENGTHWAYS
8 LARGE SWISS CHARD LEAVES, ROUGHLY CHOPPED
2 TBSP CHOPPED FRESH CORIANDER
1 TBSP CASHEW NUTS, ROUGHLY CHOPPED

1 Heat a large non-stick wok with a little sunflower oil over a high heat. Add the onion and stir-fry for about 1 minute, then add the sliced fennel and stir-fry for 2 minutes, constantly moving the vegetables around the wok with a thin wooden spatula.

2 Add the soy sauce, oyster sauce, honey, chilli sauce and the lime juice and zest and stir-fry. Toss in the asparagus and stir-fry for 2 minutes, then add the Swiss chard leaves and 1 teaspoon of water to create steam to add a little moisture to the vegetables, if required. Check the seasoning and add a little extra soy sauce if needed. Sprinkle with the fresh coriander and cashew nuts and serve immediately.

ZEST OF 1 LEMON
ZEST OF 1 LIME
1 TSP SEA SALT
700G ROOSTER POTATOES, PEELED AND ROUGHLY DICED
   INTO 3CM PIECES
3 TBSP SUNFLOWER OIL

1 Heat the oven to 230°C/fan 210°C/gas 8.

2 Combine the lemon zest, lime zest and sea salt in a small bowl. Rinse the potatoes and pat them dry.

3 Place a roasting tin in the oven with the oil and allow to heat for 3 minutes. Carefully place the potato pieces into the pan and toss them in the oil. Sprinkle with half of the lemon salt and roast for 25 minutes. Shake the pan after 10 minutes of cooking and turn the potatoes twice during the cooking time.

4 Once the potatoes are roasted and crispy, sprinkle over most or all of the remaining lemon salt, carefully toss and serve immediately.

LEMON SALT ROAST POTATOES

....

I love to serve these potatoes roughly chopped, not diced neatly or accurately, because the end result is a pile of crispy, lemony, odd-shaped, mouth-watering potatoes. Try adding 1 teaspoon of chopped fresh rosemary and add it to the lemon salt when roasting chicken and serve with a roasted garlic mayonnaise.

SERVES 4

EXTRA VIRGIN OLIVE OIL

1 LEEK, FINELY SLICED

30G BABY SPINACH

1 SMALL BUTTERNUT SQUASH, PEELED, VERY THINLY
   SLICED AND CUT TO FIT A MUFFIN TIN

3 EGGS, BEATEN

100ML CREAM

1 TSP CHOPPED FRESH THYME

SALT AND FRESHLY GROUND BLACK PEPPER

1 TBSP CHOPPED FRESH PARSLEY

12 SMALL SPRIGS OF THYME

1 Preheat the oven to 180°C/fan 160°C/gas 4. Line a 12-hole muffin tray with square pieces of parchment paper.

2 Heat a little extra virgin olive oil in a large frying pan over a medium heat and sauté the leek for 5–6 minutes, until cooked. Add the spinach to the pan and cook for 1 minute more.

3 Spoon the leek and spinach mixture into the muffin tray and layer the finely sliced butternut squash on top.

4 Whisk the eggs, cream, thyme and some salt and pepper in a jug, then carefully pour it over the butternut squash and leek layers. Sprinkle with the parsley and bake for 15–18 minutes, checking that they're cooked and set by inserting a skewer. Do not overcook.

5 Remove from the muffin tray and serve warm with sprigs of thyme on top.

BUTTERNUT SQUASH, LEEK AND SPINACH BAKES

....

Bake these the day before and just heat them 20 minutes before you're about to serve. Keep the parchment wrappers on when you serve them – the children will love them as well as grandparents! If you have any left, pack these for your lunch at the office with a refreshing rocket and pink grapefruit salad.

MAKES 12

MERINGUE CAKE WITH BLACKBERRIES AND PLUMS

....

My mum used to bake something similar to this for special occasions, and this is my version of this versatile, feather-light celebration dessert. Try it with chocolate cream in the centre or a combination of natural yoghurt, vanilla and raspberries for an even lighter version. Adding the toasted flaked almonds into the meringue gives a crispiness when you dip your fork into it. It also allows you to 'stretch' the dessert by adding extra fruit or a toffee or lime sauce. Don't be too anxious if the meringue breaks a little. It's fragile but you wouldn't be travelling around with it!

SERVES 6-8

FOR THE MERINGUE:

5 EGG WHITES
280G CASTER SUGAR
100G FLAKED ALMONDS, TOASTED
1 TBSP WHITE WINE VINEGAR

FOR THE FILLING:

8 PLUMS, HALVED, STONES REMOVED AND SLICED INTO WEDGES
100G CASTER SUGAR
1 CINNAMON STICK
3 TBSP SHERRY
2 TBSP WATER
200G BLACKBERRIES
150ML CREAM, WHIPPED WITH A LITTLE ORANGE ZEST
FRESH LEMON BALM OR MINT LEAVES, TO DECORATE

1 Preheat the oven to 190°C/fan 170°C/gas 5. Line 2 x 20cm springform tins with parchment paper.

2 Whisk the egg whites in a clean, dry bowl until stiff. While still whisking, add in half of the sugar a large spoonful at a time, then fold in the rest of the sugar all at once and whisk until the meringue is glossy and stiff. Fold in the toasted almonds and vinegar.

3 Divide the meringue between the tins. Bake for 1 hour 20 minutes and switch off the oven. Allow the meringue to cool completely in the oven, then carefully peel the parchment off the meringues.

4 Meanwhile, to make the plum filling, place the plums, sugar, cinnamon stick, sherry and water in a saucepan over a high heat. Bring to the boil, then reduce the heat to low and simmer very gently for 10–12 minutes. Remove from the heat and stir in half of the blackberries. Set aside to cool completely.

5 To assemble, place a meringue layer on a serving platter. Spread with the whipped cream and spoon over the plum and blackberry filling – make sure to only use the fruit and not the syrup. You can serve the fruit syrup in a pretty jug alongside the meringue cake.

6 Place the other meringue layer carefully on top of the filling. Decorate with the remaining blackberries and the lemon balm leaves and be proud of your achievement!

FOR THE ROASTED RHUBARB:
200G RHUBARB, CHOPPED INTO 2CM SLICES
70G CASTER SUGAR
ZEST AND JUICE OF 1 SMALL ORANGE

FOR THE CAKE:
220G BUTTER, SOFTENED, PLUS EXTRA MELTED BUTTER
  FOR GREASING
180G CASTER SUGAR
ZEST AND JUICE OF 1 ORANGE
4 EGGS
160G PLAIN FLOUR
160G GROUND ALMONDS
2 TSP BAKING POWDER
120G NATURAL YOGHURT
60ML MILK
200G RASPBERRIES
100G FLAKED ALMONDS, TOASTED
YOGHURT OR CREAM, TO SERVE

1 Preheat the oven to 180°C/fan 160°C/gas 4. Brush a 23cm springform tin with melted butter and line the base with parchment paper.

2 Place the rhubarb in a roasting tin and sprinkle over the sugar and the orange zest and juice. Roast for about 10 minutes, until just softened and cooked through. Set aside to cool.

3 Meanwhile, cream the butter and sugar together until pale and fluffy, then mix in the orange zest and juice. Add the eggs one at a time, mixing well after each addition.

4 Sieve the flour into the egg mix, then fold in the ground almonds and baking powder. Add the yoghurt and enough milk to form a soft consistency. Carefully fold in half of the raspberries, taking care not to crush them.

5 Pour the batter into the prepared tin and bake for about 40 minutes, or until firm to the touch and a skewer inserted into the centre comes out clean.

6 While the cake is still warm, place spoonfuls of the roasted rhubarb on top. Allow to cool completely, then remove from the tin. Sprinkle over the toasted flaked almonds and arrange the remaining raspberries on top. Serve with yoghurt or cream.

RASPBERRY AND ROASTED RHUBARB ALMOND CAKE

....

Rhubarb, packed with flavours and vitamins, is a firm family favourite here at Bally-knocken. Serve with natural yoghurt or vanilla ice cream.

SERVES 12

125G PLAIN FLOUR
60G CASTER SUGAR
3 TBSP COCOA POWDER
2 TSP BAKING POWDER
2 EGGS, BEATEN
50G BUTTER, MELTED, PLUS EXTRA FOR GREASING
125ML MILK
ZEST OF 1 ORANGE
GINGER ICE CREAM, TO SERVE

FOR THE TOPPING:
150G DARK BROWN SUGAR
3 TBSP COCOA POWDER
ZEST AND JUICE OF ½ ORANGE
250ML BOILING WATER

SELF-SAUCING CHOCOLATE AND ORANGE PUDDING

. . . .

This pudding looks like a mud patch in winter but it tastes likes heaven – warm, smooth, chocolaty and satisfying. Making this pudding is a bit like making those 1960s instant puddings in boxes – just add boiling water to dry ingredients!

SERVES 6

1 Brush a 22cm round ovenproof dish with melted butter.

2 Sieve the flour, caster sugar, cocoa and baking powder into a large bowl. Combine the eggs, melted butter, milk and orange zest in a large jug and mix well, then whisk into the flour mixture. Pour the pudding into the buttered ovenproof dish. Place it in the fridge and cover with plastic wrap for 5 hours.

3 Preheat the oven to 180°C/fan 160°C/gas 4.

4 Remove the pudding from the fridge. Mix together the brown sugar, cocoa powder and the orange juice and zest and sprinkle over the pudding mixture, then carefully pour over the boiling water. Bake for 40-45 minutes, until the pudding has risen and is firm in the centre. The sauce will be on the base of the crust when you break through the top. Serve with ginger ice cream.

LIME
MERINGUE
TART
· · · · · · · · · · ·

Lemon meringue pie was my
mother's speciality. It brings
back so many memories. The
lime is a delicious modern
twist on the old tradition. If
you have time, try making
these in small tartlet tins to
serve at a special gathering or
dinner party. You can even use
oranges in the filling instead
of the limes. I like to have a
soft, sweet, sticky meringue
topping – decadent, I know,
but scrummy. The lime cuts
into that rich sweetness of the
meringue topping.

SERVES 8

FOR THE PASTRY:
225G PLAIN FLOUR
3 TBSP ICING SUGAR
110G BUTTER, CHILLED AND DICED, PLUS MELTED
  BUTTER FOR GREASING
1 EGG, LIGHTLY BEATEN
1 TBSP COLD WATER

FOR THE FILLING:
5 EGGS
4 LIMES (JUICE OF 4 AND ZEST OF 1)
160G CASTER SUGAR
250ML DOUBLE CREAM

FOR THE MERINGUE TOPPING:
6 EGG WHITES, AT ROOM TEMPERATURE
360G CASTER SUGAR

1 Brush a 20cm tart tin or flan ring or a pie dish with melted butter.

2 To make the pastry, sieve the flour and icing sugar together into a bowl. Rub the butter into the flour with your fingertips until it resembles fine breadcrumbs. Mix the egg and water together, then add to the flour mixture to bind together to form a smooth pastry. Shape the dough into a ball, flatten it slightly and wrap in cling film. Rest in the fridge for at least 1 hour.

3 Preheat the oven to 200°C/fan 180°C/gas 6.

4 Lightly dust a work surface with flour and roll out the pastry until it's 4mm thick. Drape the pastry over the rolling pin to lift it over the tart tin, flan ring or pie dish. Dust off the surplus flour and unroll the pastry into the tin or dish. Gently press the pastry into the bottom and up the sides. Roll the rolling pin over the top of the ring to cut off the excess pastry. Allow to rest for 1 minute, then line with parchment paper and fill with baking beans or dried lentils.

5 Bake blind for 12 minutes, then carefully remove the beans and lining. Brush with the beaten egg and return to the oven for a further 2–3 minutes, keeping an eye on it to make sure it doesn't get too brown.

6 Reduce the oven temperature to 140°C/fan 120°C/gas 1. Mix all the filling ingredients together in a large jug, being careful not to overbeat. Pour into the pastry base and bake for 30 minutes, until set. Leave to cool.

7 When you're ready to make the meringue, preheat the oven to 180°C/fan 160°C/gas 4. Beat the egg whites in a clean, dry bowl until stiff. Add the sugar a spoonful at a time and beat until the meringue is glossy.

8 Spoon the meringue over the lime filling, lifting it into peaks. Bake for about 15 minutes, until just golden. You can also preheat your grill and pop it under the grill until just golden, but keep an eye on it. Allow to cool before serving.

CHOCOLATE, PEAR AND ROSEMARY TART

....

You'll only need a small slice of this, honest! This is also well received when you invite your friends over for some-thing sweet and serve this with coffee and your favourite liqueur.

SERVES 8

FOR THE PASTRY:
225G PLAIN FLOUR
110G BUTTER, CHILLED AND DICED
30G ICING SUGAR
1 EGG, BEATEN
1 EGG YOLK, BEATEN

FOR THE FILLING:
60G CASTER SUGAR

125ML WHITE WINE
125ML WATER
JUICE OF ½ LEMON
2 PEARS, PEELED, CORED AND THINLY SLICED
300G DARK CHOCOLATE
2 EGGS, BEATEN
220ML DOUBLE CREAM
6 SMALL ROSEMARY SPRIGS, TO DECORATE

1 To make the pastry, sieve the flour into a bowl. Add the diced butter and rub it in with your fingertips until the mixture resembles breadcrumbs. Sieve in the icing sugar and stir to combine. Mix together the egg and the egg yolk, then stir most of the egg into the flour to form a soft pastry. Shape the pastry into a ball and wrap in cling film. Place in the fridge for 20 minutes to let the dough rest before rolling it out.

2 Preheat the oven to 190°C/fan 170°C/gas 5. Butter a 20cm-long rectangular loose-bottomed tart tin.

3 Lightly dust a work surface with flour and roll out the pastry until it's slightly bigger than the tin. Line the tin with the pastry and gently prick the base with a fork without piercing through. Place in the fridge to rest for approximately 10 minutes, then line with parchment paper and fill with baking beans or rice. Place in the oven for 10–15 minutes, until fully baked. Set aside.

4 Meanwhile, to prepare the poached pears, put the sugar, white wine, water and lemon juice into a saucepan. Bring to the boil, then reduce the heat and simmer for about 10 minutes, until a thick syrup forms. Add the pear slices and simmer for 3–4 minutes, until just soft. Remove from the heat and set aside to cool.

5 Reduce the oven temperature to 170°C/fan 150°C/gas 3.

6 Place the chocolate in a bowl set over a pot of simmering water (bain marie) and melt. Whisk in the eggs and cream, taking care not to curdle the eggs, until a thick consistency is formed. Allow to cool slightly, then pour into the baked pastry shell. Bake for 15–20 minutes, until just set.

7 Allow to cool completely, then decorate with the poached pear slices and some fresh rosemary sprigs.

INDEX
....